Following Padre Pio

A Journey of Discovery from Pietrelcina to San Giovanni Rotondo

Following Padre Pio

A Journey of Discovery from
Pietrelcina to San Giovanni Rotondo

Bret Thoman, OFS

Foreword by
Adolfo Affatato

Icona Press
Peachtree City, Georgia

Following Padre Pio: A Journey of Discovery from Pietrelcina to San Giovanni Rotondo
by Bret Thoman, OFS

Copyright © 2023 by Bret Thoman.
All rights reserved.
No part of this publication may be reproduced, stored in a retrieval system, or transmitted in any way by any means – electronic, mechanical, photocopy, recording, or otherwise – without the prior permissions of the copyright holder.
Published by Icona Press.
Website: www.stfrancispilgrimages.com

Cover design by pro_ebookcovers.
Cover Photograph appears on a wall at the Capuchin friary of Venafro. It depicts an ancient map of the Capuchin friaries within the Province of Sant'Angelo. Cover photo taken by Bret Thoman.
All photographs in the book were taken by and are property of Bret Thoman.

Scripture texts in this work are taken from the New American Bible, revised edition © 2010, 1991, 1986, 1970 Confraternity of Christian Doctrine, Washington, D.C. and are used by permission of the copyright owner. All Rights Reserved. No part of the New American Bible may be reproduced in any form without permission in writing from the copyright owner.

All *Letters* excerpts taken from *Padre Pio of Pietrelcina * Letters*, Volume I (2012); Volume II (2019); and Volume III (2017) edited by Melchiorre of Pobladura and Alessandro of Ripabottoni; English Version edited by Father Gerardo Di Flumeri, O.F.M. Cap. Reprinted by permission of Edizioni Padre Pio da Pietrelcina SRL, 71013 San Giovanni Rotondo (Foggia), Italy.

This book is dedicated to all those who have devoted their lives to the Franciscan Order – friars, Poor Clares, and Tertiaries

TIMELINE

The Friaries of Padre Pios

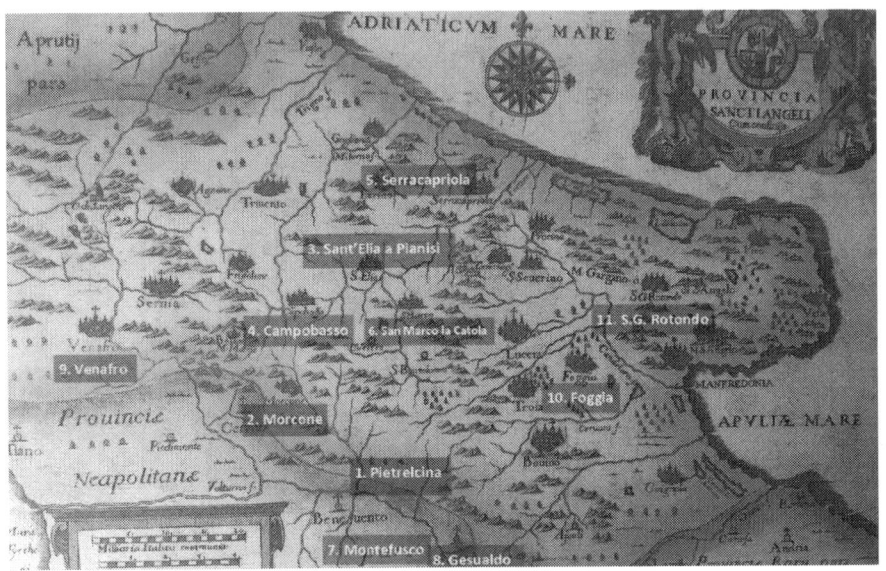

1. Pietrelcina (1887-1903; 1909-1916)

2. Morcone (1903-1904)
Francesco Forgione came to Morcone to enter the Capuchin novitiate on January 6, 1903, and was given the name, Fra Pio da Pietrelcina. At the completion of the novitiate year, he made his temporary vows here, promising to live "in obedience, with nothing of his own and in chastity (January 22, 1904).

3. Sant'Elia a Pianisi (1904-1907)
Fra Pio arrived for the first time here on the afternoon of January 25, 1904. Here he completed his rhetorical studies (1904-1905), secondary school, and philosophical studies (1906-1907).
Here he made the profession of solemn vows (January 27, 1907).

4. Campobasso (1905; 1909)

Fra Pio came to the mountain Sanctuary of the Madonna dei Monti above Campobasso twice: May 1905, to assist in a liturgy; and October 1909, for health reasons. On October 14, 1909, Pio wrote to Father Agostino: "Everything happens by the wonderful disposition of God, who wants more and more to purify our spirit to the point of making it less unworthy of himself."

5. Serracapriola (1907-1908)

In October 1907, Fra Pio came here to study sacred theology. His professor wrote that he was "good, obedient, and studious."

6. San Marco la Catola (1905-1906; 1918)

From the second half of October 1905 until the end of April 1906, Fra Pio lived here to attend the first year of philosophy. He returned as a priest from April-May, 1918 to meet with his spiritual director Father Benedetto da San Marco in Lamis.

7. Montefusco (November, 1908)

At the end of November 1908, he came here to study sacred theology. Father Paolino wrote of him: "In his whole person there is goodness and sympathy."

8. Gesualdo (November-December 1911)

Fra Pio came here briefly between November-December 1909 to study moral theology.

9. Venafro (October-December, 1911)

Ordained a little more than a year, he was in this friary from the end of October until December 7, 1911. Not being able to celebrate Holy Mass due to his illness, he received communion – his only nourishment for twenty-one days. Here mysterious events took place, such as ecstasy and diabolical harassment.

10. Foggia, Sant'Anna (1916-17)

Padre Pio left Pietrelcina for Foggia on February 17, 1916 to comfort Raffaelina Cerase, a tertiary who died on March 25, 1916. Here Padre Pio suffered due to his illnesses and the heat, and was beaten physically by the devil.

11. San Giovanni Rotondo (1916; 1918-1968)
Padre Pio came to San Giovanni Rotondo the first time on July 28, 1916 in hopes that the mountain air would be good for his health. He stayed for one week and returned to Foggia. On September 4, 1916, he was reassigned to San Giovanni Rotondo. He left on only a few occasions, such as for military service. On March 16, 1918, he returned to San Giovanni Rotondo and never left again.

If I have found favor with you, O king, and if it pleases your majesty, I ask that my life be spared, and I beg that you spare the lives of my people.

(Esther 7:3)

Table of Contents

TIMELINE vi
Foreword 13
Author's Preface 17
Acknowledgements 22
Part I: From Birth to Ordination 23
1: Pietrelcina 25
2: Vocation: to Morcone 36
3: Penance 44
4: Sant'Elia a Pianisi and Mystical Phenomena 52
5: Back to Pietrelcina, Ordination 59
In the Footsteps, Part I 67
6: In the Footsteps: Pietrelcina 68
7: In the Footsteps: Morcone, Sant'Elia a Pianisi, Campobasso 77
8: In the Footsteps: Gesualdo and Benevento 94
9: In the Footsteps: San Marco la Catola, Venafro, Serracapriola 104
Photographs Part I 116
Part II: From Ordination to Sainthood 124
10: Priesthood, Victim Soul, and Invisible Stigmata 125
11: Back to the Order, Foggia 133
12: From the Plains to the Mountains 143
13: The Permanent Stigmata 150
14: Forever in San Giovanni Rotondo 157
15: The Death and Glorification of St. Pio of Pietrelcina 178
In the Footsteps, Part II 185
16: In the Footsteps: Piana Romana 186
17: In the Footsteps: Montefusco and Foggia 192

18: In the Footsteps: San Giovanni Rotondo 203
19: In the Footsteps: St. Michael and Beyond 212
Photographs Part II 218
Afterword 227
For Further Reading 233
Books by Author 235
About the Author 237

Foreword

Adolfo Affatato –
One of the last living spiritual sons of Padre Pio

During the first few days of July 1953, my life completely changed. I was a sixteen-year-old student enrolled in a rigorous Italian *liceo* (a lyceum secondary school). The air in my hometown of Foggia was so hot that everyone was seeking refuge either at the beach or up in the hills. The infamous Favonius was blowing – that warm African wind out of the south that renders life in my native city brutal. I, too, decided to head for the hills, and went to San Giovanni Rotondo. While I was looking forward to the cooler mountain air, I also went because I had heard of a friar who could read souls and see the future. Thus, my first encounter with Padre Pio was one born solely out of curiosity… and an attempt to find out if I had passed my final exams.

I arrived in time for the Exposition of the Blessed Sacrament. The small church filled to capacity offset every benefit offered by the cooler air. While witnessing the entire service, I was struck by the intensity of the spiritual atmosphere. When I heard Padre Pio's voice, interrupted by tears, reciting the prayer of St. Alphonsus to the Virgin, I was deeply moved.

After the service, I withdrew to the small sacristy. It, too, was packed and was excruciatingly hot. Nonetheless, I was able to find some space in the rear where I stood. I remained there if for nothing else than to have the satisfaction of watching Padre Pio pass by. Finally, as was his customary ritual, he shuffled with his heavy gait toward the door on the left to return inside the enclosure. Halfway there, however, he stopped, turned around, looked in my direction, and spoke.

"Adolfo, come here."

I thought he was referring to anyone other than me as the privileged one. This was the first time I had ever visited San Giovanni Rotondo, and I had never met Padre Pio. I remained completely still. Then he repeated himself.

"Adolfo, come here."

Given his insistence, plus the fact that no one else went forward, I asked him if he were calling me.

"Is my name Adolfo?" he responded wryly, as was his custom.

With that, I made my way through the throng of people toward him. Then Padre Pio said something that has been forever etched in my memory.

"I have been waiting for you for a long time."

He then put his hand on my head, turned away, and disappeared into the cloister.

There are no words to adequately describe what I felt at that moment. It was an encounter full of joy and inner peace. Before me, I witnessed a man who radiated so much light.

Everyone present peppered me with questions, which I clearly did not know how to answer. I said that this was the first time I had ever seen Padre Pio. But this only increased their disbelief, as well as my realization that I was in the presence of someone – something – truly extraordinary. I realized in that moment that I had been called – predestined – without merit. My life was never the same after that day.

I went home, but soon returned to San Giovanni Rotondo and went to confession to Padre Pio. I was so tongue-tied, I could not speak. Instead, *il Padre* (the Father) told me my sins. I was amazed.

After my confession, I told him, "Padre, I love you."

"Evidently you do not know the love I have for you," he said to me with tears in his eyes. After he finished hearing the other confessions, he allowed me to accompany him to his cell.

He called me to him and thanked me for what I had said to him. Then he said something I have never forgotten.

"I will help and assist you until the final moment of your life."

This is who Padre Pio is.

Soon afterwards, I became his spiritual son. When *il Padre* accepted me, he said: "Of course I accept you, why do you think I called you by name that day? I was waiting for you to ask me this. But please be a worthy son, and do not make me look bad. The world is tired of words, it needs examples."

Over the following years, I had many occasions to witness firsthand the extraordinary phenomena Padre Pio is known for. And yet I am more grateful to him for having shown me the face of Christ. He was a radiant father to me.

He did for me what he did to all those he directed. He took my soul, turned it inside out like a sock, cleaned it up, and presented it to the Lord as a new creation. He removed the blindfold that prevented the light of God from shining and illuminating my earthly journey. The great soul-surgeon that he was, he removed all the scabs and scales of human misery I was carrying within. He taught me that life should not be considered a "struggle," but a continual "self-conquest" and a slow return to the House of the Father. He modeled the words of St. John, "I came that they may have life and have it more abundantly" (10:10).

Some years ago, I met an American husband and wife on the train from Foggia to Rome. They had come to San Giovanni Rotondo seeking prayers for their daughter who was going through a difficult period. They later told me about another American, named Bret, married to an Italian, who would contact me. He agreed to translate my book, *Padre Pio and I* into English. I got to know Bret in the process.

After converting to Catholicism, Bret became a Franciscan tertiary thanks to the influence of his wife. Today, they live in

Loreto, Italy near the Basilica of the Holy House of Mary, with their three children. Not only is he devoted to the Virgin Mary, he has a deep devotion to Padre Pio, whose protection and blessing he feels. When I came to America in 2019 to give conferences, Bret was my interpreter in Atlanta. What a beautiful friendship Padre Pio procured for me.

I am honored to introduce Bret's newest book, *Following Padre Pio: A Journey of Discovery from Pietrelcina to San Giovanni Rotondo*. I know it is authentic, because I know that Bret loves Padre Pio, and I know how Padre Pio uses souls to bring others to Christ.

Before he died, Padre Pio gave me a mandate. He told me to give the love he put in my heart to others. He also said: "All those to whom you speak about me, and who receive me, will enter my heart and will remain there for eternity." It is my hope that the readers of this book will know Christ's great love through Padre Pio.

Adolfo Affatato
Foggia, Italy
December 24, 2022

Author's Preface

"The Word was made flesh, and dwelt among us" (John 1:14). The Greek word translated as "dwelt" (ἐσκήνωσεν; "eskēnōsen") means, more literally, "put up his tent among us," or "tabernacled, sojourned." Drawing on Old Testament imagery (see Ex 25:8–9), within this tent or tabernacle, God would "dwell in our midst." In this poetic imagery, St. John's message is that the Word is the new mode of God's presence among his people. The tent is the world, which is now indwelt by Jesus. Christ is begotten as a man and has fully informed the world.

With Christ's Incarnation, God is no longer above us, outside, or distant. He is here, with us, present among us. This is encapsulated in the words of St. Paul: "In times past, God spoke in partial and various ways to our ancestors through the prophets," now, "in these last days, he spoke to us through a son, whom he made heir of all things and through whom he created the universe" (Hebrews 1:1-2).

The specific place where Jesus dwelled most of his earthly life was his hometown of Nazareth. He lived for some thirty years in this obscure village in the lower Galilee region – from whence one wondered if anything good could come (see John 1:46). At the age of thirty, he left Nazareth for Capernaum on the northern shore of the Sea of Galilee (see Luke 3:23), where he began to preach and call his Disciples. After a public ministry of three years, he went to Jerusalem where he endured his Passion and Crucifixion followed by the Resurrection on the third day.

Scripture reveals that most of Jesus' early life was ordinary. In Nazareth, he grew up and "was obedient to [his parents and] advanced in wisdom and age and favor before God and man" (Luke 2:51-52). Even during his ministries – in which he began publicly performing miracles and healings – he did ordinary things. He walked with his Disciples, had meals with them, and conversed. He attended weddings and was invited to people's homes. He traversed the roads of Galilee and Judea where he encountered people of different ethnicities, social classes, professions, faiths and sects, and nationalities. He taught and preached from the hills, on the plains, and along the seashore. He went to Jerusalem on pilgrimage for the important feasts. Within these mundane events and happenings, extraordinary things occurred.

It is said that one cannot fully know someone else without visiting the place where he or she grew up. At the affective level, for those who love Christ, there is something moving about walking where Jesus walked and touching his land. One feels a special closeness to Jesus after seeing the vistas his eyes gazed upon: the cliffs of Nazareth; the Sea of Tiberias; the basalt stone and rich, black soil of the fertile Galilee; the heights of Golan; the craggy peaks of Mt. Arbel beyond the Roman city of Tiberias; and the ancient streets of Jerusalem. Listening to the waves of the sea, smelling perfumes like nard, and even tasting local foods is a powerful experience.

As anyone who has been on a pilgrimage to the Holy Land can attest, visiting the places where Jesus lived leads to a more profound understanding of the Scriptures. St. Jerome referred to the Holy Land as the Fifth Gospel: "Five gospels record the life of Jesus. Four you will find in books and the one you will find in the land they call Holy. Read the fifth gospel and the world of the four will open to you." Indeed, after a visit to the Holy Land, one never hears the Gospels in quite the same way.

Like Christ who was formed in a very human way in his hometown of Nazareth, the saints, too, led human lives. They were not formed in a vacuum. In their own hometowns – among parents and relatives, educators and catechists, friends and companions – their personalities, minds, and spiritualities were formed. They are people, and they have their personal story. Padre Pio was no exception.

In this work, I have attempted to understand the life of the great stigmatized saint in a novel way: by personally exploring all the friaries where he lived. While most devotees of St. Padre Pio limit their visits to San Giovanni Rotondo and occasionally venture out to Pietrelcina, the reality is that he was the progeny of a people. Padre Pio was formed by those of his native town, as well as the friars of the Capuchin Province he entered. Just as Christians explore the Holy Land to know Christ more intimately, I have visited Padre Pio's friaries to understand him better.

For the drafting of this book, I followed Padre Pio's life trajectory from his birth and childhood in Pietrelcina, through his entrance into the Capuchin Order and various assignments throughout the vast Province of Sant'Angelo and Foggia, and finally to San Giovanni Rotondo where he lived for five decades. I stayed in Pietrelcina for five days, and from there I set out each morning to explore several sites each day.

My excursions began in Morcone, where the future Padre Pio entered the novitiate in 1903. After making first vows, he was sent to Sant'Elia a Pianisi to begin his studies. The next ten years were spent among various friaries throughout the vast Province interspersed with stints back home at Pietrelcina for health reasons: the Sanctuary of the Madonna dei Monti in Campobasso (1905); San Marco la Catola (1905-1906); Serracapriola (1907-1908); Montefusco (autumn-winter, 1908); Gesualdo (1911); Venafro (October-December 7, 1911); and Foggia (1916). Finally, he ascended the Gargano Promontory where he would live in the rural friary outside of San Giovanni Rotondo. There he would remain for fifty years until his death on September 23, 1968.

My experience visiting the friaries of Padre Pio was a true adventure. I arrived at each site in the blind without having contacted anyone. As the journey unfolded, there were no shortage of difficulties as I logged over 1,500 kilometers (930 mi) on my vehicle. The three Italian regions that make up the Capuchin Province of Padre Pio have always struggled economically (massive waves of emigrants left these areas for North and South America in the first half of the twentieth century) and the roads are often potholed or even washed out. I wondered at times if I – my car, more properly – was going to make it. Moreover, most of the friaries are situated in remote locations well off the beaten path and were frustratingly difficult to find.

Yet, *Deo gratias!*, as in the Christian life, the disappointments and concerns were tempered with many more abundant blessings. I was delighted to discover that all the cells where Padre Pio lived have been preserved with vintage furnishings to make them look exactly like they were in the early twentieth century. Additionally, each site boasts a small museum with relics and artefacts from his life. I took numerous photographs, many of which are published in this volume. Yet, the most memorable aspect of my journey was the rich encounters with the friars, sisters, and laypersons I met along the way – including some who knew Padre Pio personally. Their testimonies and stories were the highlight of my journey.

My pilgrimage in the footsteps of Padre Pio brought to life this great saint of the twentieth century in a way I had not imagined. While I knew a little about the saint, he came to life for me. But the pilgrimage also brought to light other elements of his life. My pilgrimage was like a journey in the Paschal Mystery. Just as Christ suffered, died, and was resurrected, I discovered this in the life of Padre Pio – and personally. While I anticipated some difficulties, I did not expect others. But in all of it, my faith was strengthened as I came to know Padre Pio more deeply. This was the journey of a lifetime for me, and I hope it will be for you, too.

Author's Notes:

In the Italian and other Latin languages, the word *convento* (convent), refers to a religious house where non-cloistered men or women religious (friars or sisters) live. It derives from Latin *conventus*, meaning to "convene" or "come together." Historically, its meaning was exclusively related to men's religious houses where mendicants (Franciscans, Dominicans, Carmelites, and Augustinians) – who spent much of their time travelling – came together in community. Conversely, men's or women's religious houses, in which monks or nuns were cloistered, were referred to as monasteries.

In English usage, since about the nineteenth century, the term "convent" has come to refer predominantly to religious houses for sisters and nuns, while "monastery" is used for cloistered monks; likewise, "friary" has come to be the preferred term for religious houses for mendicant men. In this book, the term "convent" is used according to the classical and Italian usage; that is, interchangeably with "friary" – and both refer to Capuchin religious houses for friars.

Regarding the difference between Brother and Father, all Franciscan friars are brothers (the word "friar" means brother), while those who are ordained are also fathers. In this book, I use the Italian titles. For brother, I use *Fra'* (short for *Frate*; that is, friar or brother) and *Padre* for Father.

Lastly, to enhance the visits to the friaries described in this book, I have included a number of photographs. There are many more on my website:

http://www.stfrancispilgrimages.com/the-convents-of-padre-pio.html

Acknowledgements

It is said that a book is written not by an individual, but by a community. That is the case regarding this book.

I would like to thank most of all everyone I met on my journey in the footsteps of Padre Pio. Each of the friars, sisters, and laypersons I encountered along the way contributed to this work directly and indirectly.

A special thank you is due to the Capuchin Province of Sant'Angelo and Padre Pio who endeavored to carefully preserve the memory of St. Padre Pio in the various friaries throughout the Province. They graciously welcomed me and accompanied me to the cells and museums of Padre Pio.

I am particularly grateful to: Father Emidio Cappabianca, Brother Donato Ramolo, Father Denis Lobo, and Brother Raffaele Armiento. Thank you for showing me your friaries, as well as the face of Padre Pio in the process. Thank you to Sr. Maria Villani for your accompaniment and your deep devotion and dedication to Padre Pio and his teachings.

Thank you, Adolfo Affatato, for your warm friendship, your indefatigable ministry as an apostle of Padre Pio, and for extending to me the love that Padre Pio put in your heart. Thank you, Anna Maria Marrone and Mario Caruso, for your dedication to the Convents of Padre Pio.

Finally, I would like to thank the readers for this book: Michelle Heekin, Maria Calandra of the National Centre for Padre Pio in Barto, Pennsylvania and Fr. Christopher Iwancio, OFM. Cap., for your extensive input and suggestions.

Part I: From Birth to Ordination

1: Pietrelcina

Our story begins in Pietrelcina – a formerly obscure village in Southern Italy. On May 25, 1887, at 5:00 PM, Grazio Forgione and Maria Giuseppa De Nunzio had just come in from the countryside to their one-room home atop the *murgia* – the harsh, rocky outcrop on which the village sat. There, in the ancient district in the midst of a ruined castle, on Vico Storto Valle, 27, a child came to light. They called him Francesco.

The closest city was Benevento, just twelve kilometers (7 mi) away. Naples lay another sixty kilometers (37 mi) beyond that. Until only a quarter century earlier, Naples had been the capital of an eponymous kingdom for centuries. From there, kings enthroned in lavish palaces ruled over all of Southern Italy. Naples was a center of culture, arts, and learning and was esteemed by the other great European courts. Now, since 1861, Italy was unified and Naples was another capital city within the Kingdom of Italy.

The concept of a united Italy had been decades in the making. Emblazoned by a nationalistic spirit, figures like Garibaldi, Mazzini, and Cavour launched what was known as the Risorgimento. From Turin in Northern Italy, they marched south with their armies to reunite the Italian peninsula under one flag. The strongest resistance came from the pope. Pope

Pius IX would not agree to surrender the territories of the Church that had been governed temporally by the papacy for over one thousand years. The Italian Kingdom responded by declaring a decree, in 1866, ordering the Suppression of the Catholic Church and the religious orders. The pope held out for ten years, but his small papal army was no match for the modern Italian *bersaglieri*. On September 20, 1871, Italian troops breeched the Roman city gate of Porta Pia and established Rome as the new capital of the Kingdom of Italy. Pope Pius responded by closing himself in the Vatican walls as a prisoner. The Suppression of the Catholic Church was complete.

The Risorgimento was the fruit of the enlightened mentality that dominated thought in the nineteenth century. An italic peninsula governed by a hodgepodge of city-states, kingdoms, fiefdoms, and foreign rule – especially papal – was not consistent with the rationalist zeitgeist undergirding contemporary thought. Italy had to modernize and be homogenous like the nations north of the Alps. Medieval ideas and religion had to be stamped out.

The 1800s were also marked by important technological and scientific advances that revolutionized society and culture. In medicine, the nineteenth century was referred to as "the great sanitary awakening," as the invention of the microscope led to advances in germ and cell theory, while vaccines were beginning to eradicate diseases. Transportation – the domain of horses and carriages and sailing ships from time immemorial – had grown exponentially due to the steam engine and expanding rail network. By the time Francesco Forgione was born in the latter half of the century, the combustible engine, light bulb, telephone, typewriter, and phonograph had recently been invented, while the radio, automobile, and airplane were not far behind.

While the world was trudging ahead toward its happy destiny, something otherworldly was about to happen in this poor, farming village in the countryside far from the important cities of Naples and Rome. Pietrelcina – practically untouched by the progress and modernity taking place in the great cities of Europe – would soon become synonymous with one of the most mystical and charismatic saints of the modern era and perhaps of all time. As one wondered whether "anything good could come from Nazareth" (see John 1:46), backwater Pietrelcina would become the scene of a spiritual battle that would spill out into the open, with signs and wonders abounding all around.

The name of the village in dialect, Pretapucina, derives from *preta* (priest) + *pucina* (hen). According to an ancient tradition, a stone sculpture of a hen and her chicks once adorned the parish church of Sant'Anna. Its contemporary name, Pietrelcina (*pietra*, stone) derives from the town's origin as a castle built on a large rock, known as the *murgia*. Unlike so many other Italian towns and cities that have roots in ancient Roman, Etruscan, or Greek times, Pietrelcina traces its origins to the High Middle Ages. During the Norman-Lombard period of the eleventh and twelfth centuries, it served as a *castrum* (castle), which eventually expanded into a settlement and then a village. The castle church was dedicated to St. Michael the Archangel, as the Lombards called on the holy warrior angel to defend them and protect them in battle. Over the centuries, due to earthquakes, wars, pestilence, and migration, the population waxed and waned. At its height in the year 1900, there were just over 4,000 residents. Today, according to the town website, 2,800 people live in the municipality.

Francesco was the fourth born child. Sadly, his parents had previously lost two children: their first-born child, also named Francesco, who died nineteen days after birth, and Amalia, who died at twenty months. Only Michele, who was then five years old, was living. Three daughters would follow Francesco.

Francesco's parents were illiterate farmers. Sometimes called Orazio, or more affectionately Zi' 'Razio (Uncle Orazio), the future saint's father was known for a cheerful and jesting personality. He was witty and always ready with a good joke. He spoke not in Italian, but in his native dialect of Pietrelcina. He was thin and of short stature, though medium height in relation to other men of his era. In photographs, he has penetrating eyes, a piercing gaze, and a serene, dignified air about him. Though he had a rugged manner and rough, calloused hands, he was sensitive. The original biographies relate that he once avoided stepping on an ant, saying, "Poor little creature, why should it have to die?"

Francesco's mother was known for her intelligence, hospitality, and strong faith. In photographs, she appears slim with a graceful countenance. She is always wearing a freshly washed, ironed kerchief over her head, as was custom among women in her milieu. She has the serene mien of someone who lived a difficult life, but did so graced by an other-worldly solace. While she was still alive, she would greet admirers of her son who frequently came to Pietrelcina to see where the popular friar was born. Though she spoke in her town dialect – a foreign language to those who traveled distances to Pietrelcina – she told stories about young Francesco with such grace and simplicity that everyone understood her.

Due to the elevated risk of infant mortality, just thirteen hours after his birth, Orazio took his newborn son a few steps away to the church of Sant'Anna (St. Anne's) to be baptized. The priest was Don Giuseppe Orlando. His parents entrusted their son to the protection of the great saint of Assisi, St. Francis, baptizing him with the name, Francesco. Sant'Anna was in a state of disrepair when the future saint was baptized, though it had been rebuilt in 1700 after an earthquake on June 5, 1688.

Within this tranquil setting of Pietrelcina – made up of people, churches, shops, and land – the future saint was born and grew to maturity. As a boy, Francesco played in the ancient neighborhood among little alleyways, stone stairs, and tiny passages atop the rocky *murgia*. Summers in Pietrelcina were excruciatingly hot and dry, while winters – with their biting cold and whipping winds – were harsh. The townspeople ate and shared what they had and always gave thanks whether the harvest was abundant or meager.

There was an earthiness and grittiness about the local people, traits the future Padre Pio never lost. The people were curt and direct, though generous and good-natured. Though they had little materially, they were content. To the future Padre Pio, they had everything. While reminiscing about his home town, Padre Pio would later say, "No one ever had ten lire in their pocket. Yet, nothing was lacking."

Though the later priest and confessor of San Giovanni Rotondo was known for being brusque (and even for an occasional outburst), such character traits were not unusual in his home town. His people were hardworking farmers and shepherds. Though they were lighthearted, they were serious. The fact is that time was limited and precious. His parents had no time to waste on folly or capriciousness. Likewise, Padre Pio knew when people before him were wasting his time, and he would not hesitate to be abrupt in such circumstances. Even while keeping adulating crowds away from him, the future Padre Pio would drive them away with the cord around his waist as if herding a flock of sheep. He never lost his rural ways.

Some compare Padre Pio's strong temperament to the stone foundation of his town and the permanence of the former castle settlement. It not only signed him psychologically, but also spiritually. Indeed, he would draw on God as his rock throughout his life – especially during the excruciatingly difficult period of his persecution. Certainly, the fervent religiosity of the people formed him. The people of Pietrelcina were known for their devotion to the angels and saints, frequent prayers in their fields and houses, and the religious festivities and customs. Religious holidays were scrupulously observed with local customs and pageantry – especially the first Sunday of August. On that day, the Madonna della Libera – the patron saint of Pietrelcina – was celebrated with a traditional procession of her statue through the village.

Like his parents, young Francesco also spoke the dialect of the *Pucinari* (the name for the locals of Pietrelcina) and also referred to his town as *Pretapucina*. He continued to speak the vernacular language (which was similar to the Neapolitan dialect) throughout his life, and he often used popular sayings. He once told a spiritual son that it was easier to express his thoughts better in dialect. Many expressions do not translate well into Italian, let alone English. Once, a shoemaker from Pietrelcina visited him in San Giovanni Rotondo. Padre Pio told Vincenzo, "Hey 'Cienz', let us both make shoes so that people can walk *straight*." The word he used in dialect, *dridd'*, (*dritto* in Italian), means "straight" both in Italian and dialect. But in dialect, it also means "well" as in "straight and narrow," giving his quip a moral connotation.

Francesco Forgione spent much of his childhood in the countryside in an area known as Piana Romana, about two kilometers (1.3 mi) from town. Padre Pio's parents were not sharecroppers, they were landowners, even if the plot of land they owned was small. In Piana Romana, Orazio and Maria Giuseppa owned a small farmhouse (known as a *masseria*) and two hectares (five acres) of land. From town, Orazio would saddle his donkey early and set out from Pietrelcina into the countryside. His wife, Zi' Giuseppa or Mamma Peppa, assisted with the farm work and prepared meals. When their children were old enough, they, too, helped out in the fields.

Young Francesco was tasked by his father to tend to the sheep. Often he banded together with companions who were also shepherds. Francesco played with his friends and relatives, but was also known for his seriousness. One companion recounted how meticulous he was with the bread and jam given to him by his mother. While his friends took their breakfast in a sloppy manner, Francesco ate it almost ceremoniously. He gave thanks for the bread as if it were given to him directly by God.

At home, Francesco attended Mass daily with his siblings and mother, prayed the Rosary nightly, and abstained from meat on Fridays, Saturdays, and Wednesdays in honor of Our Lady of Mount Carmel. In the cold months, his parents and grandparents told Bible stories to the children in the evening as they huddled around the fire to keep warm.

When he was with his friends at school or at recreation, Francesco appeared like everyone else, though he stood out for his religiosity, cheerfulness, and maturity. He was ordinary, if slightly reserved and introspective. He spoke so little, his companions gave him a nickname, *lup' surd'* (deaf wolf). The reality is that he was uncomfortable around boys who cursed or misbehaved. If the other boys swore or blasphemed, he was visibly pained.

Francesco's mother said he was a good boy and always obedient. She said he never misbehaved and always obeyed her and Grazio. She never needed to discipline him with anything more than an occasional scolding for his petty arguments with his sisters. Padre Pio himself later confirmed this by saying that he was never spanked, though he was occasionally reprimanded for playing pranks on his sister, especially Felicita, of whom he was particularly fond. They had no indoor plumbing in those days — just basins for spot washing. When Felicita would wash her face and hair, he would sometimes come up behind her and dunk her face in the basin. Instead of getting angry, she would smile and say, "Franci, when will you ever give up playing pranks on me?"

On September 27, 1899, at the age of eleven, Francesco received the sacrament of Confirmation. The Mass was celebrated in the church of Sant'Anna by the Archbishop of Benevento, Msgr. Donato Maria Dell'Olio. Padre Pio later referred to that day as the "most singular and most unforgettable day of my whole life." He also received his First Communion in St. Anne's.

The little church near his home was vitally important to his spiritual development. There he attended catechism and learned the basic elements of Christian doctrine. He also served as an altar boy. Sometimes, Francesco would remain in the church after the doors were closed and locked. The sacristan would agree on a set time in which he would return and unlock the door so Francesco could leave. He would spend hours in prayer on his knees before the Blessed Sacrament. He would sometimes go into ecstasy.

At the tender age of five, Francesco received his calling to be a priest in that church. On one sweltering summer afternoon, he saw Jesus appear next to the main altar. Christ gestured for Francesco to approach him, and he put his hand on the boy's head. The future priest and saint understood that sign as a choice, a calling. He became aware of God's approval and love for him. Without hesitation, he gave his assent. He proposed in his heart that he would consecrate himself and give himself completely to God.

Before entering the seminary, Francesco would need to be educated and be able to read Latin. Schooling was neither compulsory nor free in those days, so his parents would have to pay for it personally. Initially, Francesco was tutored by a local farmer who was literate, but not well educated. So he switched and went to a private school run by a laicized priest named Domenico Tizzano. His initial studies in Latin and other subjects began badly, and Tizzano was not impressed by the future saint. He told Francesco's mother that he was an *asino* (a donkey), but she didn't believe him. She took him to another private teacher named Angelo Caccavo, who subjected

Francesco to an interrogation. This time, he did well. (Some suggest that Francesco did poorly with Tizzano, due to the fact that he was an ex-priest.)

Though his tutors were not exorbitantly expensive, Francesco's father needed more resources. For this reason, he emigrated to America so as to afford to send his son to school. He went first to Uruguay, then to Brazil. (Italians refer to North and South America as a single continent.) Orazio's wife shared the sacrifice in that she was now forced to take on the double burden of caring for her children alone and working the fields in Piana Romana.

Francesco took his schooling seriously, knowing that he could not be ordained if he did not have a rudimentary academic foundation. During this period, he often sought solace in a room atop what he referred to as *La Torretta* (the Tower). He would go there to study in silence and dedicate himself to contemplation and private prayer. He stayed in touch with his father in America via correspondence. Once, Angelo Caccavo took the boys to Pompeii on a scholastic excursion. Francesco wrote to his father telling him that though the excursion would incur an expense, he would soon abandon this life to embrace another one, one infinitely better.

While Francesco knew he would be transformed upon ordination, it is unclear if he understood just how exceptional his priestly life and ministry would be. On August 25, 1896, something took place in a neighboring village that foreshadowed the mysterious events that would surround his life. Early that morning, Orazio and his nine-year-old son set out from Pietrelcina on their mule-driven carriage to the town of Altavilla Irpina, some twenty-seven kilometers (17 mi) away. It was an important holiday – the feast day of San Pellegrino, an ancient Roman martyr and city's patron saint known for thaumaturgical miracles and healings.

At the end of the Mass, pilgrims remained in the sanctuary to implore the saint for intercessions. Among the faithful was a young mother who begged San Pellegrino to heal her deformed son whom she was holding in her arms. Orazio got up to leave, disturbed by the commotion and wailing, but Francesco wished to remain. He joined his prayers to those of the desperate woman and remained in deep intercessory prayer.

Finally, the mother threw her son on the altar in desperation, shouting: "If you won't heal him, take him back!" To the astonishment of everyone present, the child stood up and walked. He was completely healed. The mother couldn't believe her eyes. Everyone in the sanctuary cried out, praising and thanking God for the miracle that had taken place. Francesco Forgione was also struck by what happened. Though he already had a strong interior life, this was the first time he witnessed such a healing. Many observers of the life of Padre Pio consider this moment to be an announcement of the mysterious things God would accomplish through the future Padre Pio.

In addition to his developing prayer life, Francesco also began practicing corporal disciplines. He would frequently sleep on the floor using a stone for a pillow. Don Giuseppe Orlando, the parish priest of Pietrelcina, once reprimanded Francesco for not sleeping in his bed, which his mother had prepared. But Francesco responded that he wanted to "suffer like Jesus." He also sometimes used a cord for self-flagellation. Ubaldo Vecchiarino – one of his companions from the countryside – said that he and his friends would spy on Francesco during the winter months. They would sneak up to his house silently and place stones under the window to see what he was up to. Though the room was dark, they could hear the blows of someone striking himself with a hemp cord. His mother testified that she saw him disciplining his body. She asked him once why he did it, to which he replied, "I must beat myself just as the Jews beat Jesus and made his shoulders bleed." She was stunned at his response and never questioned him again when she heard him self-flagellating. Though she understood the spiritual practice, it pained her deeply.

From the age of five, Francesco began experiencing spiritual visions. It is no coincidence that the demons began appearing and trying to torment the child after he felt the calling to the priesthood. They would appear in obscene, human or bestial forms. Alternately, Francesco was consoled with visions of angels, saints, and other heavenly figures. During moments of celestial apparitions, he would go into ecstasy. He did not speak about these phenomena because he believed everyone experienced them. Padre Agostino of San Marco in Lamis, his future spiritual director, learned of them in 1915, when Padre Pio was twenty-eight years old. He wrote in his Diary:

> The ecstasies and apparitions began at the age of five when he first had the idea of consecrating himself forever to the Lord, and they were continuous. When asked why he had kept them hidden for so long [until 1915], he candidly replied that he had not disclosed them as he believed they were ordinary things which happened to all souls. In fact, one day he naively said: "You don't see the Madonna?" To my negative reply, he added: "You only say that out of holy humility." At the age of five, diabolical apparitions also began, and for almost twenty years, they were always in the most obscene forms: human and above all bestial.

Within this brief portrait of the early years of Francesco Forgione, certain aspects of his spirituality are already evident – especially regarding his embrace of penance. This is apparent in his love for prayer and solitude, his sense of recollected devotion, his love of the sacraments, his aversion to immorality and iniquity, his respect for and obedience to his parents and elders, and his embrace of asceticism and corporal disciplines. Within this context, the young Francesco would soon discover the fullness of his vocation: a priesthood consumed in suffering and expiation for the redemption of sinful souls and for the healing and relief of suffering humanity. His journey into the Paschal Mystery had begun.

2: Vocation: to Morcone

A vocation begins within one's heart and soul as a personal, intimate invitation from God to draw closer to him and serve him and others in an exclusive manner. Often it begins as a gentle longing, usually a quiet whisper, though sometimes it can be a powerful, driving force. While some hear their calling in external, audible voices or experience some other extraordinary sign, most experience it as an inner voice speaking to their soul.

Francesco Forgione, the future Padre Pio, was among those who felt his calling as a small child. As has been recounted, at the age of five, he had a heavenly vision in which Christ appeared to him in the church of Sant'Anna. While he knew he wanted to be a priest, the kind of priest he would become would be revealed later.

Around the age of ten, Francesco was with his parents in the countryside of Piana Romana threshing when his attention was struck by the presence of a bearded friar coming over the hill. He was dressed in a long, brown tunic with a pointy hood over his head. Around his waist was a white cord with three knots. He was begging alms in what is known as the *questua*. His name was Fra' Camillo da Sant'Elia a Pianisi and he was stationed at the nearby convent of Morcone. He was a Capuchin friar.

The kindly Fra' Camillo gazed down at the boy with serene eyes set within a rosy face and a long, black beard. With a smile and a caress, he handed Francesco a religious medal. Mamma Peppa smiled at his generosity and responded by filling his cart with alms. For almost four centuries, the Capuchin friars had a reciprocal relationship with the townspeople: the friars served the laypersons spiritually who, in turn, took care of the religious materially. Both benefitted from the other. After blessing the family, the friar disappeared down the hill toward the village of Pietrelcina.

There in the tranquil countryside of Piana Romana, the Lord spoke to the heart of Francesco. The seed was planted. He wanted to become a "monk with a beard," like Fra' Camillo of Sant'Elia a Pianisi. He desired to become a Capuchin.

The Capuchin Order was, and is, one of three Franciscan obediences, known as the First Orders. St. Francis of Assisi founded just one order known simply as the Order of Friars Minor, which eventually split into the Order of Friars Minor (formerly the Observants) and the Order of Friars Minor Conventuals. The Capuchin Order separated from the Observant branch in 1528.

St. Francis was born in Assisi during the winter of 1181-82. His father, Pietro di Bernardone, was away in France buying cloth during his birth. His mother, Pica, had him baptized and named Giovanni (John) in honor of the Baptist. When Pietro returned from France, he began calling his son Francesco, after the land of France, where he made his money and worked as a merchant.

As a young man, Francis lived a carefree life and dreamed of increasing his social position by becoming a knight. While en route to fight in a crusade, God appeared to him in a dream and asked Francis if it was better to serve the Lord or the servant. Recognizing the voice of the true Lord, Francis realized he had not been seeking the will of God in his life. He renounced war, gave away his armor and weapons, and returned to Assisi.

Francis began praying in caves and rebuilding churches. In a pivotal moment, he embraced a leper. He wrote in his spiritual Testament that this moment marked the beginning of his penance – his conversion. He soon left the security of his father's house and adopted poverty as a way of life. From that moment, he lived as a mendicant and penitent. Others began following him, and the brothers received approval from Pope Innocent III. The charism of the order, based on poverty, led the pope to designate the title of the fledgling movement: the Order of Friars Minor (Lesser Brothers).

For the next twenty years, Francis traveled throughout Italy and beyond preaching penance, working for peace, performing miracles, serving lepers, and praying in hermitages. The Franciscan way of living the Gospel had an explosive impact on the culture and religion of the era. By the end of Francis's life, thousands of men had become friars. In 1212, St. Clare became his first female follower, and soon after, women's religious communities everywhere began to imitate her Franciscan way of life from within the cloister. At the same time, lay men and women began turning to Francis seeking spiritual guidance, and he soon formed the Third Order (today known as the Secular Franciscan Order) – a movement for laypersons who wished to follow Franciscan spirituality from within their own homes.

Toward the end of his life, Francis retired to the mountain of Laverna, near Arezzo in Tuscany. During a fast in honor of the Feast of St. Michael the Archangel, on September 17, he received the stigmata – the wounds of Christ – on his hands, feet, and side. Two years later, on the night between October 3-4, 1226, he died peacefully in Assisi. Two years after that, he was canonized a saint by Pope Gregory IX.

After St. Francis's death, the order he founded began to separate. One group of friars continued striving to live the rigorous way of life intended by the founder. They lived in the hermitages outside the cities, prayed uninterruptedly, and practiced harsh penances and corporal asceticism. They were eventually labeled the Observants, as they were seeking to "observe" the Rule of St. Francis without gloss. On the other hand, another group began mitigating the rule and its austere way of life. They tended to be intellectuals and theologians and were called to important ecclesiastical positions within the Church. They were known as the Conventuals, due to the large convents they lived in within the city walls. By the early sixteenth century, the two groups had become irreconcilable. Therefore, in 1517, Pope Leo X officially separated the order into the Observant and Conventual Franciscan branches.

The Capuchin Order began soon thereafter. In the 1520s, within the hills near the ducal city of Camerino in central Italy, a small group of Observant Franciscans felt a desire to live an even harsher

Franciscan life based on solitude, hermitage, and even more austere penance. With the support of the duchess of Camerino, Caterina Cibo (whose uncle was Pope Clement VII), the new movement received papal approval on July 3, 1528. The friars became known as the "Capuchins" due to their unique capuches, or hoods. In line with the monastic tradition, they grew long beards (as a sign of austerity.)

Attracting followers through their preaching, prayer, austerity, and service among the poor, the new movement grew rapidly and spread in all directions. In 1530, friars ventured from Camerino and founded a hermitage in the Gargano Mountains (in northern Puglia) on the Adriatic Sea near the famed sanctuary of St. Michael. Other sites were founded in Foggia, and the order continued spreading inland. Eventually, the Capuchin Province of Sant'Angelo-Foggia was established.

This was the Province of Fra' Camillo, and this is the order that attracted young Francesco Forgione.

After Fra' Camillo left, Francesco said to his parents: "I want to become a monk like that one with the beard." Initially, they objected and tried to persuade him to join a different community. Mamma Peppa knew how rigorous the Capuchin Order was, and she suggested he become a Benedictine monk at the Abbey of Montevergine, which was nearby. His father said he should consider becoming a friar in Paduli, a neighboring village where Franciscan friars of the Observance staffed a church and convent. Life in either of those orders would be much less austere for Francesco whose health was already feeble.

"No," said Francesco, "I want to become a bearded monk."

While the early biographies do not indicate what it was about Fra' Camillo that struck him – other than his beard – Francesco probably sensed something else. Perhaps there was something in Camillo's gaze or there was some spiritual quality about him that drew Francesco and led him to believe that he, too, was called to become a Capuchin priest. He may have been able to "read" the soul of Fra' Camillo and see the radical embrace of the cross that marked his order. Whatever it was, he was attracted to Fra' Camillo. He wanted to become a Capuchin.

When Francesco was fifteen, his parents took him to speak to the superiors of the convent of Morcone – the nearest Capuchin community and the site of the novitiate for the Province. It was necessary to be at least fifteen years old and have no impediments. Francesco qualified. However, there was no space available then. He would have to wait. In the meantime, he would continue his studies with Angelo Caccavo, with whom he had already completed three years of secondary school.

Francesco's sacrifices and commitment were not long in waiting. In the fall of 1902, good news reached Pietrelcina. A spot had opened up in the novitiate. His entrance was set for Epiphany, January 6. The news was a source of boundless joy for Francesco and his family, but it was also a source of suffering and trial.

Francesco's parents were supportive of his entrance into religious life. However, the reality is that he was still a minor. He was just fifteen years old, well below twenty-one, the age of *maggiore età*, or the legal age of adulthood in that era. Though Orazio and Giuseppina supported him wholeheartedly – his father emigrated to South America so as to educate him! – there were affectionate and filial bonds that were about to be broken. Yet, this was the norm. Young vocations were typical in that era. Adolescents called to religious life or priesthood often entered high school (minor) seminaries run by the orders they planned to enter. The 1917 Code of Canon Law described the purpose of minor seminaries as: "to take care specially to protect from the contagion of the world, to train in piety, to imbue with the rudiments of literary studies, and to foster in them the seed of a divine vocation."

Though it was commonplace, it was painful – for parents, as well as children. Francesco experienced his imminent separation as an indecision whether to remain "in the world" or leave it. Though he had desired to be a priest for years, he was now beginning to have doubts as to whether or not he could actually go through with it. He was about to undergo his first battle.

As he prepared for his departure, Francesco had a series of three visions. Under holy obedience, Padre Pio later wrote about them and what he experienced just prior to his entrance into the novitiate. The texts were written by Padre Pio himself and are included in the autobiographical notes in the first volume of *Letters of Padre Pio*.

In the first vision, Francesco foresaw his future as a continuous and bitter struggle against the enemy. This vision was decisive in his resolution "to bid farewell to the world and devote himself entirely to God in a sacred enclosure." He did not indicate when the vision took place, only that it was during a period in which he "began to drink great draughts of this world's vanity." He wrote that his soul was wrestling with the "increasingly strong vocation on the one hand and a sweet but false delight in the things of the world on the other."

While meditating on his vocation and "wondering how he could make up his mind to bid farewell to the world in order to devote himself entirely to God in a holy enclosure," he was suddenly rapt from his senses and drawn to see "with the eye of his intellect," objects different than what one sees with the eyes of the body. Referring to himself as a soul in the third person, he saw:

> a majestic figure of rare beauty, radiant as the sun. This man took him by the hand and he heard him say: "Come with me, for it is fitting that you fight as a valiant warrior." He led him to a vast plain, where there was a great multitude of people, divided into two groups. On one side he saw men of beautiful countenance, clad in snow-white garments; on the other, in the second group, were black-robed men of hideous appearance who seemed like dark shadows. Between these two large groups was a wide space in which that soul was placed by his guide. As he gazed intently at the two groups, suddenly, in the middle of that space which separated them, a man advanced, so tall that his forehead touched the clouds, while his countenance was that of a hideous black monster. At this sight, the poor soul was completely disconcerted and felt his life suspended. The strange figure advanced nearer and the guide at the side of that soul informed him that he would have to fight this individual. At these words the poor thing turned pale, trembled all over and was on the point of

falling to the ground in a faint, so great was the terror he experienced.

[…]

[God speaking:] "All resistance is useless; it is advisable that you fight this man. Take heart; enter confidently into the combat, go forward courageously, for I shall be close to you. I will assist you and not allow him to overcome you. In reward for your victory over him, I'll give you a splendid crown to adorn your head."

The poor soul took heart and entered into combat with that dreadful and mysterious being. The impact was tremendous, but with the aid of his guide who never left his side, he finally overcame his adversary, threw him to the ground and obliged him to flee. (*Letters*, Vol. I, pp. 1426-28 - Edizioni Padre Pio da Pietrelcina, 2012)

The second vision took place five days prior to his entrance into religious life; that is, on the Feast of the Circumcision of the Lord, January 1. It helped him better understand the meaning of the first vision. Padre Pio wrote:

He had received Holy Communion and was engaged in intimate converse with his Lord when his soul was suddenly flooded with supernatural light. By means of this most pure light he understood in a flash that his entry into religion in the service of the heavenly King meant being exposed to combat with that mysterious being from hell with whom he had fought in the previous vision. (*Letters*, Vol. I, p. 1429 - Edizioni Padre Pio da Pietrelcina, 2012)

Finally, the night before he was to leave his home and enter the novitiate, he had another more prominent vision, one he described only very briefly. This third vision was given to him on behalf of

Jesus and Our Lady exclusively for consolation and encouragement. He wrote that he was still suffering in "the lower part of his soul" due to the separation from his family members, to whom he felt strongly united, and he felt in this abandonment "even his bones being crushed" to the point that he might faint. He saw Jesus and his Mother who in all their majesty began to encourage him and to assure him of their predilection. Finally, Jesus placed his hand on Francesco's head, which was enough to make him strong in the "higher part of his soul" so that he would "shed not a single tear at this painful leave-taking, although at that moment he was suffering agonies in soul and body." (*Letters*, Vol. I, p. 1430 - Edizioni Padre Pio da Pietrelcina, 2012)

The day of Francesco Forgione's departure was January 6, 1903, four months shy of his sixteenth birthday. At the train station in Pietrelcina, the separation was difficult. His mother wept, even though she had surrendered her son to St. Francis with all her heart. Francesco felt pained, too, but he was resolute. Indeed, he did not shed a single tear. The visions had strengthened him. He knew what he was called to and felt consolation in the profound love of God and Our Lady. He smiled and bade his mother farewell.

His teacher, Maestro Caccavo, and his parish priest, Don Nicola Caruso, joined Francesco on the train to his new home. The friary was in Morcone, some twenty-seven kilometers (17 mi) to the north of Pietrelcina. It was the site of the Capuchin novitiate of the Province of Sant'Angelo-Foggia (today known as the Province of Sant'Angelo and Padre Pio).

The train ride took less than one hour. After they arrived at the station in Morcone, in the plains below the old town perched on the steep mountain, Francesco and his two chaperones walked 1.5 kilometers (1 mi) to the convent located in the countryside just below the old city. Francesco pulled the rope attached to a bell inside the cloister. To his delight, he was greeted by Fra' Camillo – the same begging friar whose beard inspired him so many years earlier in Piana Romana. Fra' Camillo greeted him with a delightful smile and a customary kiss and embrace.

"*Bravo, bravo,* Francì! You have been faithful to the promise and call of St. Francis!" he said. Francesco returned his smile. He then said his farewell to his teacher and parish priest, crossed the threshold, and Fra' Camillo closed the door behind him. He had now left the world and entered religion.

3: Penance

Once in the convent, Francesco Forgione was introduced to the others who had also just arrived, as well as to Padre Tommaso da Monte Sant'Angelo, the novice master, who was known for being severe. He immediately subjected the boys to an examination. All passed. One of them, however, was not yet fifteen years of age and had to leave. Another would leave after a few days once he realized just how harsh Capuchin life really was.

Francesco was shown to his cell. Initially, he was assigned to cell no. 18 in the corridor for novices. Later, he would relocate to cell no. 28 – in the other novice corridor. The cells in the novitiate were small and sparsely furnished. They consisted of a narrow bed with a lumpy mattress stuffed with corn leaves resting on a metal plank, a chair and small desk for study, and a wash basin.

The first week was spent in strict silence, as required by the Capuchin Rule. A reminder of the calling, *silentium*, was painted in Latin on a sign on the corridor in the novitiate. The novitiate was a place of recollection. In fact, for Francesco and the others called to be there, silence was not deadening, it was life-giving. Only by listening could they hear God speak. And for those who were listening, there was much to hear and learn: "Listen, my son, and receive my words, and the years of your life shall be many" (Proverbs 4:10).

In those days, it was customary for those entering the Capuchin Order (and other orders) to receive a new name. Their baptismal names and paternal surnames were substituted with a religious name followed by the city of their birth and baptism. The change of name signifies one's new life and new identity; the old man is cast aside, the new man put on. The son of Orazio and Maria Giuseppa would no longer be known as Francesco Forgione, but from then on by Fra' Pio da Pietrelcina – Brother Pio. His new name – Pius, in English – was chosen by the novice director in honor of St. Pius V and St. Pius the Martyr (whose relics were preserved in the church of Sant'Anna in Pietrelcina).

Sixteen days after Fra' Pio's entrance into the order, with the period of silence and spiritual exercises completed, the trial had ended. He easily passed. From the day of his entrance, his superiors and the professed friars in the permanent community were struck by Pio's humility and his willing obedience. He would always reply to them by saying simply: "Yes, Father." Often he didn't even finish his sentence before he was already carrying out what he had been ordered to do. He was now invited to progress to the sacred vestition.

The Rite of Investiture – in which the postulants received the Capuchin habit and officially became novices – was a beatific moment for young Pio. The date was January 22, 1903. On that day, Fra' Pio kneeled down before the main altar of the convent church to receive his new tunic. The habit has particular meaning, as it is linked to a fuller, more conscious adhesion to Christian life. For Franciscans, the habit has penitential meaning. With the arms extended, the habit is in the form of a Tau-shaped cross, and is, thus, associated with conversion and the Passion of Christ. Francis of Assisi viewed it as a tangible sign for his friars in identification with the crucifix.

According to the Rule of St. Francis, the donning of the common habit signifies insertion into the community: "Let those who have promised obedience take one tunic with a hood" (*Later Rule*, 2, 14). Likewise one's ouster, or exclaustration, is determined by depriving the friar of the tunic, which symbolizes the order: "Let him be deprived of the habit he has lost by his wickedness, put it aside completely, and be altogether expelled from our Order" (*Earlier Rule*, 13, 1).

Padre Tommaso performed the Rite of Investiture: "May the Lord vest you as the new man, who, according to God, is created in justice and in the holiness of truth."

Handing Pio the capuche – the hood – he added an invocation: "Place, Lord, the hood of salvation on his head to defeat the diabolical snares."

Finally, he placed on Pio the cincture with another exhortation: "May the Lord gird you with the cord of purity, and extinguish the mood of lust from your loins, so that the virtue of continence and chastity may remain in you."

With that, Fra' Pio was officially a novice and advanced to the next phase of formation. Life in the novitiate was more rigorous than the young novices had imagined, including Fra' Pio. Apart from the demanding schedule for study and meditation, the Capuchin Order was decisively more penitential than the Observant and Conventual Franciscan Orders. It would be a true test. Despite the difficulties, Pio had been given the virtue of fortitude to remain. He was called.

Penances included the frigid winter air (there was no source of heat), frequent fasting, and the interruption of sleep due to the recitation of night prayer from midnight to 1:00 AM. Silence was important, too. When walking about, the novices were required to keep their heads lowered, with their gaze fixed on the ground and hood up, so as not to be distracted by the things of the world. In this way, they would preserve an inner recollection and maintain mastery over the senses. While sleeping the few hours they were permitted, they were to lie on the bed in supine position with a simple, wooden crucifix on their chest clutched in their hands. They were not to roll over. In this way, they were to resemble a corpse in a coffin, as if they had died to themselves. Most penitential of all was the practice known as the "disciplines." Three days a week, the novices would follow the novice master into the chapel. In the darkness, they would pull up their tunics and flog their bare backs with an iron chain.

Fra' Pio's mother visited Pio in Morcone on the one day allotted for family visitations. She went away stunned. Not only did he appear emaciated, Fra' Pio would not speak to her or even look at her. Instead, he kept his gaze fixed on the floor. Horrified, she believed something was terribly wrong, he was sick, or that he had become brainwashed or indoctrinated. When Grazio learned of what their son had become, he went straight to Morcone to take him out of there. But the novice director explained that penance was part of Capuchin life and Fra' Pio was precise in his obedience according to the rule.

Franciscans practiced strict penances in imitation of the founder of the order. St. Francis wore a hair-shirt (a rough wool or horsehair garment) under the habit directly on his skin. He fasted excessively and when he did eat, he mixed his food with ashes or bitter herbs to kill the taste. He slept little, often using stones as pillows. He responded to temptation by disrobing and rolling around in the snow or in thorn bushes, and he, too, flogged his body.

St. Francis did all this in an effort to discipline his body, or flesh. He wrote, "All who love the Lord with their whole heart, with their whole soul and mind, with all their strength, and love their neighbors as themselves and hate their bodies with their vices and sins, and receive the Body and Blood of our Lord Jesus Christ, and produce worthy fruits of penance" (*Second Letter to the Faithful*).

In this, he was following Scripture literally: "But I say, walk by the Spirit, and do not gratify the desires of the flesh. For the desires of the flesh are against the Spirit, and the desires of the Spirit are against the flesh; for these are opposed to each other" (Galatians 5:16-17). For this reason, he often referred to his body as "Brother donkey;" that is, its stubbornness needed to be dealt with harshly. Through self-mortifications, St. Francis was seeking to detach himself from the desires of the flesh and the pleasures of the world. It was a way to counter the inordinate desire for pleasure and comfort and the natural tendencies inclined towards selfishness and self-centeredness. He wished to die of the things of the world in order to be filled with the things of God.

Though life in the novitiate was harsh, Fra' Pio took joy in his penances. He even requested more. He felt joy when the novice master would call the novices together for the "disciplines." He did not mind sleeping little on the hard, lumpy mattress, laboring in the fields behind the convent, and the long prayer vigils. Instead, as he later wrote, he was: "immensely happy when I suffer, and if the impulses of my heart consent, I would like to ask Jesus to give me all the suffering of men."

He spent most of his time in silence and prayer. During recreation time, while the others would go out, Fra' Pio chose, instead, to remain in the choir or his cell to pray – always with the permission of his superiors. If a fellow novice wished to speak with him, he conveyed his thoughts with gestures and facial expressions. He didn't do so due to an introverted character; on the contrary, he always got along well with others.

The asceticism practiced in his early formation would have a lifelong effect on Pio. Through penance, his body would become a "living sacrifice" (see Romans 12:1). In the flesh, he would "fill up what is lacking in the afflictions of Christ" (see Colossians 1:24). He would "pick up his cross and follow Jesus" (see Mark 8:34). Pio was learning to offer his penances (which included the illnesses he had been afflicted with since childhood) to the sacrifice of the cross. He was beginning to demonstrate an understanding of the mystical calling he had: a sharing in the Paschal Mystery – the life, death, and resurrection of Jesus Christ.

Fra' Pio was convinced that he had found his calling in this life. If he had any doubts before entering the novitiate, they were now gone. In a later letter to his spiritual daughter, Nina Campanile, dated November 26, 1922, he wrote about his experience in the novitiate:

> He seemed to call me to another life. He let me understand that the safe port, the haven of peace was in the ranks of the ecclesiastical militia. Where better could I serve you, O Lord, if not in the cloister, under the banner of the Poor One of Assisi? [...] May [God] grant me the grace of making me a less unworthy son of Saint Francis, so that I can be an example to my confrères, in order that fervor might continue to grow more and more within me, making me a perfect Capuchin. (*Letters*, Vol. III, pp. 1015, 1018 - Edizioni Padre Pio da Pietrelcina, 2017)

If Fra' Pio believed he had found his calling, so did his fellow novices and superiors. Their testimonies about Pio and his time in the novitiate are glowing. A fellow novice who arrived a few months after Pio said, "He was exact in everything. ... He was always docile and respectful to the voice of the superiors, and with the usual reply of 'Yes, Father,' he was on his way to carry out whatever was asked of him." Padre Tommaso, the novice director, echoed this notion. Though he was frequently critical of the novices, he had nothing but positive things to say about Brother Pio. He said that he considered him to be "exemplary, punctual in observance, and precise in everything," so much so that he never had the slightest reason to reproach him. He also said that he was "an example to everyone."

If Fra' Pio had any weakness at all during his novitiate, it was his studies. He did not stand out for intellectual aptitude. On the other hand, he was always prepared. Some said he spent little time studying. But this is because he spent most of his personal time on his knees praying.

At the conclusion of the year of formation, the novices were invited to make a week of spiritual exercises, after which time they were interrogated. The superiors wanted to ascertain that they were choosing sincerely and freely and that they understood what Capuchin life entailed. After confirming Fra' Pio possessed the requisite knowledge of religion and the Capuchin rule, the commission of friars from the Province of Sant'Angelo and Foggia continued with their questioning.

"Are the vows you are about to say spontaneous, sincere, without threat, effort, or coercion of any person of the world or of religion?"

"Yes," responded Fra' Pio.

"Do you intend to commit yourself to God with the three vows, observing the life and the rule of the Capuchin Friars Minor in perfect community life?"

"Yes," he responded once again.

With that, he was admitted to profession. Fra' Pio and the other novices could make their temporary profession. The Mass was set for Friday, January 22, exactly one year after the Mass of Investiture. In the presence of his parents and the entire community, the young Fra'

Pio professed what were known as simple, or temporary, vows. He promised to live in obedience, poverty and chastity, observing the rule of the Capuchin Friars Minor.

Presiding over the Mass and representing the Capuchin Order of Friars Minor, was Padre Francesco Maria da Sant'Elia a Pianisi, the guardian of the community of Morcone.

The formula of profession was succinct. When it was his turn, Fra' Pio read it in Latin:

> I, Brother Pio da Pietrelcina,
> steadfast in faith and will,
> vow and promise to Almighty God the Father, to blessed Mary always virgin, to blessed Father St. Francis, to all saints and to you, Father Francesco Maria,
> to live for three years, that is until January 22, 1907
> in obedience, without anything of my own, and in chastity.
>
> At the same time, I profess to observe the life and Rule of the Friars Minor,
> confirmed by Pope Honorius,
> promising to observe it faithfully
> in accordance with the Constitutions of the Order of the Capuchin Friars Minor.
>
> Therefore I entrust myself with all my heart to this brotherhood,
> so that by the working of the Holy Spirit,
> after the example of Mary Immaculate,
> and through the intercession of our Father Francis,
> and of all the saints,
> with the help of my brothers,
> I may constantly strive for the fullness of love
> in the service of God, of the Church, and of all people.

To these words, the guardian added: "If you will observe these things, I promise you eternal life."

Having made his simple vows at Morcone, Fra' Pio was now fully a Capuchin friar. He no longer wore the scapular over his tunic, as was the custom reserved for novices. Three knots were added to the cord around his waist symbolizing poverty, chastity, and obedience. He would spend the next three years maturing his vocation and, if he still felt called and if the community accepted him, he would make permanent vows. But first, he would continue his studies.

4: Sant'Elia a Pianisi and Mystical Phenomena

On the morning of January 25, 1904, Fra' Pio and Fra' Anastasio da Roio left Morcone to begin studies. They were accompanied by the Provincial Minister, Padre Pio da Benevento, on the fifty-kilometer (31 mi) journey to Sant'Elia a Pianisi. Located on a high ridge, Pio would join the other students already in the *studentato*, or Capuchin seminary for more studies and solace in what was known as the *ginnasio*, or studies of rhetoric (1904-1905) followed by philosophy (1906-1907).

In Sant'Elia a Pianisi, Fra' Pio became acquainted with the life of Padre Raffaele da Sant'Elia a Pianisi – a saintly Capuchin friar who died three years before Pio arrived. He was born on December 14, 1816 and died in the convent in Sant'Elia on the feast of the Epiphany, January 6, 1901. Raffaele was considered a model for the young Capuchin friars to emulate. He was renowned for his humility, quiet simplicity, and deep devotion to the Capuchin way of life. Some said they witnessed him rise up in ecstasy, while others witnessed him speak with the Virgin "in a loud voice and with the confidence of a son." (Raffaele da Sant'Elia a Pianisi was proclaimed "venerable" on April 8, 2019.)

Later in his life, Padre Pio wrote a tribute for the holy friar:

> O chosen and innocent soul, Father Raffaele, I am not worthy to have been chosen as one of those who knew the

pilgrimage of your earthly life. But I thank God for granting me the grace to know the perfume of your virtue. Your life captures my mind and heart; may it please God to enable me to imitate you even to the smallest degree.

Now that you enjoy the vision of God, pray for me and the Province so that your spirit and that of the Seraphic Father may always radiate from each of his Brothers. (San Giovanni Rotondo, April 5, 1956)

In the above eulogy, Padre Pio had the experience of age and wisdom. But when he was a young student in Sant'Elia a Pianisi, he was suffering from scruples and doubts. The more the young Fra' Pio tried to follow in the footsteps of the saintly Raffaele, the more his mind focused on his own foibles and weaknesses. He was tormented by two principal doubts: Not being sure he had confessed all the sins of his past life and whether or not he had confessed them well; and, in relation to the constant temptations against holy purity: Not being sure if at the first assault of the enemy, he was ready to resist. This was the beginning of the terrible torment of his soul, which he referred to as a martyrdom of scruples, and which lasted four years.

The torments were such that Fra' Pio considered leaving Italy. In May, 1904, the Minister General of the order, Padre Bernard da Andermatt, came to Sant'Elia a Pianisi for a visitation. Young Pio used that occasion to request a transfer abroad as a missionary, believing that living in the missions in Northern Africa would relieve him of his torment. Perhaps sensing the wrong motives, the Minister General denied his request.

If Fra' Pio was struggling with scruples in Sant'Elia a Pianisi, the other students and professed friars did not notice. Nor were they aware of the beatific visions that began to multiply during this period. Instead, Pio appeared an ordinary member of the community just like the other students and aspirants. He took part in recreation, weekly walks, and scholastic trips. He was outgoing and participated in the community. He was always humble and reflective. If anything, he was recognized as a model of exemplary behavior.

What was taking place within his innermost self was revealed years later. On September 30, 1915, Padre Agostino da San Marco in Lamis, his future spiritual director, wrote to him wishing to know two things: 1) "When did Jesus begin to favor you with his heavenly visions? 2) Has he granted you the ineffable gift of his holy stigmata, although invisible? Has he allowed you to experience, and how often, his Crowning with Thorns and his Scourging?" (*Letters*, Vol. I, p. 735 - Edizioni Padre Pio da Pietrelcina, 2012) In a letter dated October 10, he responded to the first question, stating that the visions began not long after entering the novitiate.

In Padre Agostino's next letter, dated October 13, he asked five more questions including when and where his scruples began. Four days later, Padre Pio responded that they lasted from the time he was eighteen and continued until the end of his twenty-first year. During the first two years, he added, this trial was almost unbearable. He wrote that it took place when he was "in Sant'Elia and later, in San Marco la Catola, and elsewhere."

While he was suffering from scrupulosity, his visions became more pronounced. He had at least two supernatural visions in Sant'Elia a Pianisi. He experienced a "strange" event and an "unusual" event. The "strange event" took place one year after he arrived, that is, on the evening of January 18, 1905. While Fra' Pio was in choir praying with Fra' Anastasio, he suddenly found himself in an upper-class home in which he saw a girl being born in one room, while her father was dying in another. This is considered the first bilocation of Padre Pio.

The father was Giovanni Battista Rizzani, a wealthy marquis in the northern Italian region of Udine. His wife was Leonilde Serrao, and the girl was named Giovanna. Leonilde later said that during her labor, she saw a Capuchin friar in front of her and walking in the corridors of the house.

Fra' Pio wrote about what he saw while he was in Sant'Elia a Pianisi:

> I was in choir with Fra' Anastasio, at about 11:00 PM. I found myself far away in a stately home, where the father

died, while a child was born. Then Mary most holy appeared to me and said to me: "I entrust this creature to you. She is a precious stone in a raw state. Work her, polish her, make her as bright as possible, because one day I want to be adorned with her."

"How will it be possible, if I am still a poor cleric and I do not even know if one day I will have the good fortune and joy of becoming a priest? And even if I am a priest, how can I think of this little girl, since I am very far from there?"

But Our Lady added: "Do not doubt, it will be she who will come to you. But prior to this, you will meet her in St. Peter's."

After that I found myself in the choir again.

Giovanna and her mother moved to Rome in 1922. While visiting St. Peter's, she felt moved to go to confession. She entered one of the confessionals staffed by a Capuchin friar. It was Padre Pio, though Giovanna did not know who he was. He heard her confession in bilocation. The following year, Giovanna heard of Padre Pio for the first time. Following a prompting of the spirit, she went on a pilgrimage to San Giovanni Rotondo.

Giovanna later recalled her meeting with the stigmatized friar. She said:

> At the small convent of San Giovanni Rotondo, there were many people. The corridor leading from the sacristy to the cloister was crowded. I managed to find a spot in the first row. As he passed, Padre Pio stopped in front of me. He looked into my eyes and said to me, smiling: "Giovanna, I know you. You were born the same day your father died."
>
> The next morning, I went to confession. As soon as I approached him, Padre Pio blessed me and said: "My

> daughter, you have finally come. I have been waiting for you for many years. Last year on a summer afternoon, you went with a friend to St. Peter's Basilica in search of a priest who could enlighten your doubts about the faith. You met a Capuchin and talked to him for a long time. That Capuchin was me."

> After a short pause, Padre Pio continued: "When you were about to be born, Our Lady allowed me to witness the death of your father, and then she told me to take care of you. You have been entrusted to me by the Virgin, and I must think of your soul."

Giovanna asked Padre Pio if she should become a nun, to which he said no. She would enter the Third Order of St. Francis. Later, Padre Pio gave her a new name, Sister Jacopa. From that moment, she became his spiritual daughter. She married, had a Christian family, and frequented Padre Pio for the rest of her life.

The "unusual event" experienced by Fra' Pio during his stay in Sant'Elia a Pianisi included a diabolical vision. The devil revealed himself to Fra' Pio in the form of a hideous, black dog. The event took place during the summer in 1905. Padre Pio later recounted the event:

> I was in Sant'Elia a Pianisi during the period of study of philosophy. My cell was the penultimate one in the corridor, which runs behind the church, at the height of the niche of the Immaculate Conception, which dominates the façade of the main altar. One summer night, after the morning recitation [recited upon rising, before dawn], I had the window and the door open due to the great heat, when I heard noises that seemed to come from the neighboring cell. "What is Fra' Anastasio doing at this time?" I wondered. Thinking that he was awake in prayer, I began to recite the Holy Rosary. In fact, we had a contest to see who would pray more, and I did not want him to get ahead. However, as these

noises were continuing more insistently, I went to call my confrere. Meanwhile, I smelled a strong odor of sulfur. I leaned out of the window to call him – our two windows were so close that we could exchange books or anything else merely by reaching out. " Fra' Anastasio, Fra' Anastasio," I tried to call him without raising my voice too much. Receiving no response, I withdrew from the window, but with terror I saw a large dog enter the door, from whose mouth was emitting a great deal of smoke. I fell on my bed and I heard him say [in dialect]: *"E' iss', è isso."* (It is he, it is he). While I was in that posture, I saw the animal jump on the window sill, from there throw itself on the roof in front, and then disappear.

In addition to his scruples and apparitions, Fra' Pio began to suffer physically. On an outing with the superior and other students, they had been guests of the community of Sant'Onofrio staffed by the Friars Minor (formerly known as the Observants) in the town of Casacalenda some twenty kilometers (12 mi) away. They were making their way back to Sant'Elia a Pianisi when they got caught out in a violent storm. Completely soaked, they decided to turn back to Casacalenda.

When they arrived back at the Observants' friary, they were given towels to dry off and a fire was lit in the hearth. Padre Isidoro, one of the Minors, saw that Fra' Pio seemed more frail than the others, and he loaned him his dry tunic. Unfortunately, his generosity was not enough. Fra' Pio caught a cold and developed a cough.

From that moment onward, Fra' Pio began experiencing ill health that would mark the rest of his life. He suffered from a host of ailments including chronic breathing problems, bronchitis, and asthma, in addition to fevers, vomiting, and regurgitation. While some speculate that his poor health was caused by, or at least aggravated by, his ascetic penances, others believe it was part of his particular calling. Padre Pio's illnesses were not strictly physical in nature. There was something otherworldly to them.

In October, 1905, Fra' Pio and the other students were forced to leave Sant'Elia a Pianisi due to renovation work on the church and other structures in the complex, and they were sent to the convent of San Marco la Catola near Foggia. There they would continue minor and philosophical studies. After six months, they returned to Sant'Elia a Pianisi.

After completing philosophy studies, Fra' Pio confirmed his adherence to religious life in the Capuchin Order forever. The date was Sunday, January 27, 1907 when he promised perpetual profession to the Capuchin Rule of St. Francis. The formula of perpetual vows was virtually identical to the one he had made three years earlier at the conclusion of the novitiate in Morcone. The difference was that these vows would last for life.

Now Fra' Pio was, in his own words, "forever linked with the vows of the Capuchin Order, under the Rule of the Seraphic Father, St. Francis, of one and only purpose: to attend to the good of my soul and to dedicate myself entirely to the service of God."

5: Back to Pietrelcina, Ordination

Over the following decade, Pio would be constantly on the move, both for studies and health reasons. After his initial formation in Morcone and Sant'Elia a Pianisi, he was sent to San Marco la Catola on October 9, 1907 for philosophy exams. Later that month, he was reassigned to Serracapriola to begin studies in theology. One of his teachers was the intellectual Father Agostino da San Marco in Lamis. Their relationship would prove important, as Padre Agostino would become his second spiritual director over the following years marked by illness and inner turmoil.

His other spiritual director was Padre Benedetto, also from San Marco in Lamis. Fra' Pio met him in October, 1905, during the six-month period in which he was in San Marco la Catola while the convent in Sant'Elia a Pianisi was being renovated. At just thirty-four years old, Padre Benedetto had already served in leadership positions within the Province. He was esteemed by friars from both inside and outside the Province due to his reputation for wisdom and prudence. He was initially a definitor – a member of the Provincial Minister's council – but would be elected Provincial Minister in 1909, an office he would serve in for ten years until 1919. This period would coincide with Padre Pio's absence from the order and cause Padre Benedetto numerous difficulties.

The exchange of letters between Padre Pio and his two spiritual directors comprise the entirety of the first volume of the *Letters of Padre Pio*, the four-volume set of letters written by and to Padre Pio. In these missives between Pio and his two directors, Pio reveals his innermost thoughts and feelings during his early life as a friar and priest. His two directors strived to discern what was underlying the intense suffering and consolations he was enduring physically and spiritually. Padre Agostino, more than Padre Benedetto (who was Pio's superior, as well as his spiritual director), was the first to recognize that the phenomena surrounding Pio's life were not natural.

Also in Serracapriola, Fra' Pio became acquainted with the life of a saintly friar in the order's history from centuries earlier: Padre Matteo d'Agnone (1563-1616). Not only was he a learned teacher and powerful preacher, he also served as Provincial Minister. But he was better known for his spiritual gifts, including prophecy and discernment, and for his remarkable prayer life during which he sometimes went into ecstasy. However, he is most known for his ministry of casting out demons. It is believed he performed some 650 exorcisms in his lifetime. He died while in the convent of Serracapriola on October 31, 1616, and his tomb remains there today. He has been declared a Servant of God, and his cause of beatification is underway.

After Pio's brief assignment in Serracapriola, he continued his pilgrimage through the various convents of the Province of Sant'Angelo scattered throughout the regions of Puglia, Campania and Molise. In November, 1908, he was transferred to Montefusco, in near Avellino, to continue his studies in theology. During the months of November-December 1909, he was sent to Gesualdo to study moral theology. He also spent a few months in the convent in Venafro from the end of October through December 7, 1911. Not much is made of these minor places where Pio lived during this part of his formation, as he spent so little time in these friaries. What seems more pressing on Fra' Pio and his spiritual directors – and can be drawn from their letters – is what was taking place within.

In the cathedral of Benevento on December 19, 1908 Fra' Pio received minor orders; that is, acolyte, exorcist, lector, and porter. Two days later, he was ordained to the subdiaconate. (In 1972, Pope Paul VI suppressed the minor orders and transferred the role of subdeacon to that of acolyte.) Sadly, Pio was unable to take much delight in these two important moments. By now, his illnesses were becoming debilitating. Since his initial ailment the prior year in Casacalenda, religious life was becoming increasingly difficult. His maladies were preventing him from participating in community life as they often rendered him bedridden.

Doctors who examined him were unable to recommend anything other than "a little air" in his hometown. Thus, in May, 1909, Fra' Pio returned to his native village of Pietrelcina for the first time after entering the order in 1903. What should have been a brief stint back home to recuperate ended up lasting almost seven years. He would not leave Pietrelcina permanently until February, 1916.

Though Fra' Pio – and his superiors – wondered what was going to become of him (to the point that there was doubt if he would be able to remain in the order), a divine plan was underway. During this period, a mystical woman from San Giovanni Rotondo had a vision foreseeing his arrival in the Capuchin convent. In 1906, while absorbed in prayer, Lucia Fiorentino (1889-1934), saw the arrival of her future spiritual father ten years before he arrived. In 1929, as part of an autobiography, she wrote:

> In the vision I saw a tree of immeasurable size in the vestibule of our Capuchin Friary and I heard a voice say to me: "This is the symbol of a soul which is now far away, but will come here. He will do a great deal of good in this village.... He will be strong and will have strong roots like this tree, and all those souls who come — both from here and from far away — if they take refuge in the shade of this tree, will be freed from evil; that is, whoever comes to this worthy priest for enlightenment, to find forgiveness and to make amends for their sins. If they humble themselves, they will receive advice and fruits of eternal life from this worthy priest. Woe to those who despise his advice, his behavior; the Lord will severely punish them in this life and the next. His mission will extend throughout the whole world, and many will come to take refuge in the shadow of this mystical tree, in order to receive the fruits of grace and forgiveness." (*Letters*,

Vol. III, pp. 474-475 - Edizioni Padre Pio da Pietrelcina, 2017)

But "who knows God's counsel, or who can conceive what the Lord intends?" (Wisdom 9:13). Often God's will and plans are not revealed immediately. They are worked out in time and understood in prayer and discernment (as well as in facts and circumstances). Certainly neither Fra' Pio, nor his two spiritual directors, could have seen the prodigious plans that God had in store for the future Padre Pio in San Giovanni Rotondo. Instead, he was back home in Pietrelcina.

Initially, Padre Benedetto did not object to Pio returning home. He gave him permission to continue his studies in preparation for sacerdotal ordination, to the best of his ability, while he kept him and Father Agostino updated. Fra' Pio took lessons from an elderly priest from his hometown, Don Giuseppe Orlando, so as not to postpone ordination. However, it soon became apparent that his health was not improving. At home, he felt better, but was still not completely well.

Doctors were never able to clearly diagnose his physical maladies. What began as a simple cold soon affected his breathing and prevented him from eating. The most frequent diagnosis was that of bronchopneumonia – a type of pneumonia that causes inflammation in the alveoli. Those inflicted with this respiratory ailment have trouble breathing because their airways are constricted; due to inflammation, the lungs do not get enough air. Yet, Pio's was a peculiar form of bronchopneumonia. It was relentless in that he would go into remission only to have his lungs flare up again. Symptoms included fever, sweating, vomiting, and excruciating chest pains whenever he coughed.

As time went by, his absence from the convent began to create not a few problems within the order, especially with Padre Benedetto. He was not only Pio's spiritual director, he was his superior. Living within a community was, and is, a cardinal aspect of the Franciscan, and Capuchin, way of life. While temporary absences from religious life could be granted for fully professed friars easily by one's

Provincial Minister, a long-term absence would necessitate special permission from the highest authorities.

According to the Constitutions of the Capuchin Order, a solemnly professed friar may not leave the order but for very serious reasons. In order to do so, he would have to present his petition to the Minister General, who would have to forward it, along with his opinion and that of his Definitory, to the Holy See, to whom alone is reserved the concession of such an indult (see Constitutions, 340). Being fully aware of the issues surrounding Fra' Pio's de facto exclaustration, Padre Benedetto repeatedly called Pio back into the convent. A cursory reading of the letter exchange between the two reveals a frustrated Provincial Minister. When ordered back to one convent or the other, Fra' Pio always obeyed, but invariably would be forced to return home after short periods. The one thing that benefited Fra' Pio's health was being in Pietrelcina. There his health would improve, though he never fully recovered.

If Fra' Pio's absence from the order was causing trouble for his superiors, Pio himself took no delight in it, either. He felt ashamed toward his confreres knowing that he was the source of so much trouble. The reality is that he had longed to become a "bearded friar" since childhood, which meant more than merely wearing the Capuchin habit (which Fra' never stopped wearing throughout his period in Pietrelcina). While he enjoyed the presence and company of his mother and family members, he longed for community life. He pined for fraternity prayer and fellowship, conventual Mass, common chores, penances, and his cell. Yet, he had no choice. When he was away from Pietrelcina, he mysteriously fell ill. It was such that he sometimes felt he was going to die.

His ill health forced him to postpone his ordination to the diaconate twice. Finally, on July 18, 1909, in the convent church of Morcone, where he had received his habit and made his temporary vows, Fra' Pio was ordained a deacon. Bishop Benedetto Della Camera, the auxiliary bishop of Telese and Cerreto Sannita, ordained him. He was then sent to Gesualdo, near Avellino, to study moral theology. But he remained only two months of November and

December. Once again, the newly ordained deacon was sent home for health reasons.

Fra' Pio continued suffering from fevers and severe vomiting that rendered him bedridden. His condition soon became unbearable, and he believed he was close to death. He prayed "to be soon released from the bonds of this miserable body." The idea of his recovery seemed "a dream" to him, and "without sense." The fever continued and the pain in his chest was unbearable. All the while, he continually invoked the intercession of Our Lady and resigned himself to his suffering believing that God was allowing it for a reason.

Fearing he might not live much longer, Fra' Pio wrote to Padre Benedetto asking him to seek permission for him be ordained at an earlier date. The main issue was related to his age. Canon law prescribes the minimum age for ordination at twenty-four. But Fra' Pio was just twenty-three. For this reason, Fra' Pio asked Padre Benedetto to request the Holy See to issue a dispensation from the age requirement. After receiving approval from the Congregation for Institutes of Consecrated Life in early July, Padre Benedetto wrote to Fra' Pio that he had obtained the dispensation. He could be ordained nine months early. Therefore, the ordination could take place around August 10 or 12, "God willing."

Padre Benedetto requested that Fra' Pio return to the convent of Morcone in the middle of the month. In a letter on the 14th, the Provincial wrote Fra' Pio that Padre Agostino would accompany him to Morcone and discuss the details of his ordination and preparation. He told him to be at peace and dismiss the afflictions and scruples which were caused by the enemy. One week later, on July 22, however, Fra' Pio wrote to his superior telling him that he was forced to return back home to Pietrelcina after just one day. He said that "after one day in Morcone I at once felt much worse, so much so that as I write I am in bed from weakness due to a return of vomiting." (*Letters*, Vol. I, p. 216 - Edizioni Padre Pio da Pietrelcina, 2012)

After he returned from Morcone, an exasperated Padre Benedetto began to accept the reality of Pio's condition. He wrote to

Fra' Pio expressing resignation regarding his absence from the order. In a letter on July 26, 1910, Padre Benedetto wrote:

> How are you now? I am sorry, but I adore the lofty decree of God who certainly, by his unspeakable compassion, does not allow you to live in that cloister to which he himself has with great condescension called you. Perhaps he wants you to be an exile in the world so that you may place all your hope and pleasure in him alone. (*Letters*, Vol. I, p. 217 - Edizioni Padre Pio da Pietrelcina, 2012)

Back in Pietrelcina, Fra' Pio's condition improved enough for him to continue studying for his examination with the aid of the parish priest. On July 30, Fra' Pio went to Benevento for his interrogation. His responses satisfied the archdiocesan commission, and he was approved. He could now be ordained.

The date of his ordination was set for August 10, 1910, the feast day of San Lorenzo, the early deacon martyr. With a heart overflowing with joy, on a hot August morning, Fra' Pio set out via carriage on the twelve-kilometer (7 mi) trip to Benevento. With him were his mother and Don Salvatore Pannullo. His father and brother, Michele, were in America working.

Fra' Pio was headed to the cathedral, the important see of the Archdiocese of Benevento. Benevento has been a bishopric since at least 305 AD and a metropolitan see since the year, 969. But according to an ancient tradition, the city's first bishop was San Fotino (St. Photine), a Greek, sent by St. Peter himself in the year, 40 AD. Built on the site of the first church in Benevento, where the Roman capitol once stood, the current cathedral dated to the Lombard foundation of the Duchy of Benevento, in the late eighth century. Unfortunately, it was bombed in 1943, and has since been rebuilt.

The ordination Mass took place in the Chapel of the Canons, to the left of the main altar. The Mass was celebrated by Monsignor Paolo Schinosi, the titular archbishop of Marcianopoli and general visitor of the metropolitan archdiocese of Benevento. The

Archbishop of Benevento, Monsignor Benedetto Bonazzi, was away temporarily. Like all priestly ordinations, the liturgy was simple, solemn, and moving. When it was time, Pio lay on the ground with his face on the floor, a Lenten gesture recalling death to self: dust to dust. He prayed to the saints, especially Our Lady, and invoked the Holy Spirit. He bowed his head as he felt the warmth of the bishop's hands on it.

Padre Pio forever remembered what he experienced at that moment. He described it in a letter to Padre Agostino, dated August 9, 1912 – two years after his ordination:

> But, my dear Father, as I write where do my thoughts fly? To the great day of my ordination. Tomorrow, the feast of St. Lawrence, is also my feast-day. I have already begun to experience again the happiness of that day which is so sacred for me. Already this morning I began to have a taste of paradise... And what will it be when we taste it for all eternity? When I compare the peace of heart I experienced on that day with the peace of heart I have begun to feel since the eve of this feast, I find no difference. On St. Lawrence's day my heart was more inflamed than ever with love for Jesus. How happy I was and how I rejoiced on that day! (*Letters*, Vol. I, pp. 335-336 - Edizioni Padre Pio da Pietrelcina, 2012)

Brother Pio would now be known by a new name, the one he is affectionately known the world over: Padre Pio (Father Pius). He was a priest forever according to the order of Melchizedek. He had received the faculty to consecrate the Eucharist, reconcile sinners, anoint the sick, and impart sacerdotal blessings. He was eternally transformed. His soul was indelibly marked with sacerdotal orders. And he would not waste time in offering these gifts to others. God would use him in extraordinary ways.

In the Footsteps, Part I

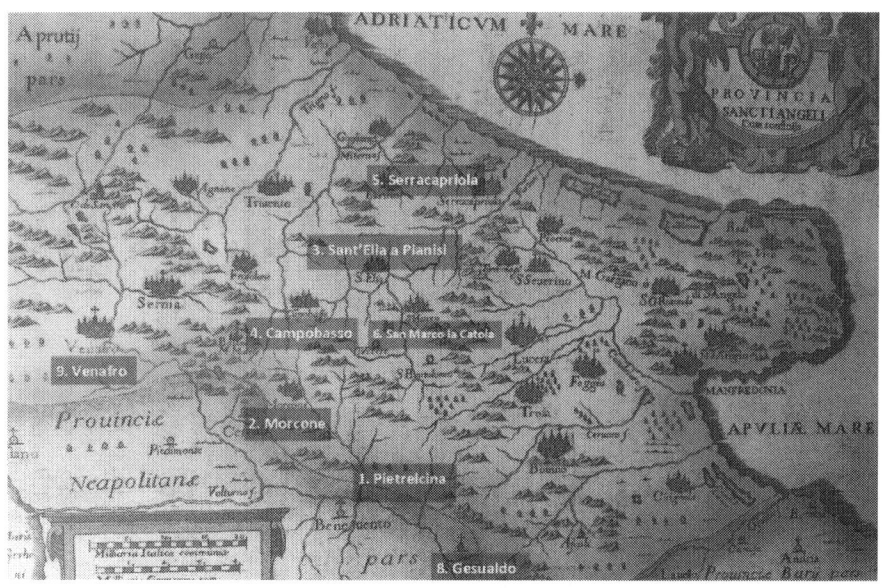

6: In the Footsteps: Pietrelcina

Having explored the life of St. Padre Pio, in the following Footstep chapters, we will explore the places connected with his life. We begin in his birth city.

Often eclipsed by San Giovanni Rotondo, the saint's lesser visited native village is a treasure trove of carefully preserved memories and sites from Padre Pio's childhood and the early part of his priesthood. Many visitors to Pietrelcina find it more faithful to the Franciscan spirit of simplicity and the charism of Padre Pio than San Giovanni Rotondo. Devoid of so many souvenir shops, swanky hotels, grandiose churches, and modern artwork, it brings pilgrims back to the era and life of Padre Pio.

The people of Pietrelcina are the "living stones" – those who have preserved the memories of Padre Pio in a unique way. Many of the elderly still speak dialect, particularly the elderly. Whether seated on park benches, gathered in the coffee bars, or yelling across the squares at one another, they speak the language that Padre Pio and his parents spoke, though it's not as sharp as it once was. I try to decipher what they are saying, but it is impossible for me. Dialects are as distinct from standard Italian as Spanish or Portuguese.

Many people here still have connections to Padre Pio. I have the pleasure of meeting a gentleman named Mario Caruso. His grandmother was born the same year as Francesco Forgione, and she lived in the countryside near Piana Romana. Mario's mother became a spiritual daughter of Padre Pio. Mario is so devoted to the saint that he created a walking itinerary connecting all the convents of Padre Pio – the same ones I will begin visiting today.

I spend some time with Anna Maria Marrone, a tour guide and representative of the tourism entity of Pietrelcina. She speaks numerous languages, including English, German, and French. She grew up in Switzerland, though her parents were from Pietrelcina. When her parents retired and moved back to Pietrelcina, she planned on going with them and staying for two years. She's now been here for twenty-five. She, too, is a wealth of knowledge of the life of Padre Pio and the people and places associated with his life. Anna Maria knew people close to Padre Pio, such as Nina Campanile from San Giovanni Rotondo – the first person to discover Padre Pio's stigmata. She married a doctor from Molise and after Padre Pio died, she went to live there. She lived to be almost 100 years old.

The people are still by and large religious. While secularization has affected the Church in other parts of Italy, de-Christianization hasn't arrived down here. I attended the parish church each day for 5:30 rosary followed by Mass. The church was full every day. And this is where we will begin our journey in the footsteps of Padre Pio: at the church of Santa Maria degli Angeli (St. Mary of the Angels).

The main church is located just off the main square, Santissima Annunziata – the former name of the parish. Destroyed by an earthquake on June 5, 1688, it was rebuilt. Today it is in perfect condition. Set to the side of the square and facing storefront property on the other side of a narrow street, it appears discreet. It isn't. The church's tall, yellow-topped bell tower – made of the same Majolica tiles (glazed ceramic) that adorns churches and buildings up and down the Amalfi Coast – makes it a prominent point of reference from anywhere in town or in the vicinity of Pietrelcina. The large, handsome, marble façade is also impressive. Though Pietrelcina is a small village, the sheer size of this parish church speaks to the religiosity of its 3,000 residents. It is clear this sanctuary has been carefully safeguarded and curated by its people.

Upon climbing the steps, after being greeted by two friendly dogs, images of Padre Pio and St. John Paul II welcome us. Eight bronze panels make up the large doors that tell the story of

Pietrelcina and Padre Pio. Just inside the vestibule are stained glass windows from an older era with more scenes from the life of Padre Pio.

The interior of the baroque-embellished church is pleasant, if a little busy. It is well-luminated with airy windows and a cream-colored ceiling and cross vaults. There are multiple side altars and niches filled with statues and saints. One of the most important is encased behind the main altar: the seventeenth-century, wooden statue of the Madonna della Libera, the patron saint of Pietrelcina. She is carefully removed from here and processed through the village for her feast day, which takes place on the first Sunday of May.

More prominent is Padre Pio. Memories and images of the great saint of Pietrelcina abound. They should. When he returned home between 1910 and 1917 due to his illnesses, his pastoral ministry was based here first as a deacon and then as a priest. Four days after his ordination, he celebrated his first Mass here. To the left side of the nave is a large, bronze statue of Padre Pio kneeling in prayer. On the right side is a large reliquary containing a glove, coagulated blood, and bits of the saint's hair. There is another statue of him – this one wooden – off the side of the altar. After spending some time in prayer (and poking around in the souvenir shop to the left of the church), I head back outside.

I exit the church, caress the head of one of the crossbreed canines at the door, descend the steps, and turn left. We are headed into the old part of town. Known as the Castle district, it sits on the rocky *murgia*, a local term used (to my knowledge) only here. I follow signs to the *Case di Padre Pio* (the Homes of Padre Pio), which consist of Francesco Forgione's birth home, as well as the places he lived as a friar: the Tower (*La Torretta*); the home of his brother, Michele, in Via Sant'Anna, 44; and the Maternal House on Via Sant'Anna, 2.

The main street – wide enough for pedestrians only (or a carriage and donkey in a bygone era) – leads into the old town. While we pass some souvenir shops, the touristy element does not feel excessive. As we get deeper into the old village, there is a more ancient feel. There are narrow, one- and two-story homes made primitively of stone, reminding visitors how people lived not all that long ago. The dwellings were constructed directly into the rock, and the natural and hewn stone blend together harmoniously. This area does have the feel of a castle. There is rock everywhere. I think of Padre Pio who said he "remembered every stone of Pietrelcina."

The street narrows further and begins to climb and wind about. There is no shortage of steps. There are some ruined, disinhibited houses alongside newly refurbished ones. I cannot help but be struck by the contrast of some boarded up houses buttressed up against an attractive B&B or a posh lawyer's studio.

On the whole, the streets and ambiance are typical of Italy's historic centers (known as *centri storici*) in every ancient city in Italy. Yet, there is something unique about Pietrelcina. Apart from the souvenir shops, foreign languages spoken, and occasional busload of pilgrims, there are plaques affixed into the walls. They are phrases from Padre Pio's letters in Italian. They are edifying. I pause and read some of them. It says, "When you are not able to walk in large strides on the way that leads to God, content yourself with small strides and wait patiently until you have legs to run, or better, wings to fly" (*Letters*, III. No. 18).

As the street starts uphill, we come to the Madonnella door. It emerges just before the entrance leading up to the most ancient part of Pietrelcina. Recessed in the wall above a door are three tiles made of Majolica, or glazed ceramic. Represented are St. Michael the Archangel, Our Lady Crowned, and St. Anthony of Padua. The guidebooks say that Padre Pio gathered in the room here with local residents for prayer meetings. The group of devotees he met with is considered the first Padre Pio prayer group.

A few steps away, on Vico Storto Valle, is *La Torretta*, the Tower. It is easy to miss. It may have been a standalone tower in the past, though it is now backed by two larger buildings. After climbing a steep staircase, a door at the top opens into a simple room, separated from the public by a low gate. Francesco came here as a boy for prayer and study. Later, he returned as a Capuchin student and as a priest from 1909-11 and continued to use this isolated space for prayer, study, and rest. Here he began writing letters to his spiritual directors from which we have intimate details of his spiritual life.

The furnishings are from the late nineteenth century and are spartan. They consist of a simple bed up against the wall on the right, a nightstand, and an old wooden desk and chair to the left by the window. Within a recessed alcove in the wall is a bookshelf consisting of two shelves lined with a handful of books. On the wall are a framed photograph of a young Padre Pio and an image of the Sacred Heart of Jesus. Above the bed is a crucifix. I admire the simplicity of the space and am grateful for the care that went into preserving the room as it looked when our saint was here.

We descend the stairs and continue uphill. After less than one minute, we come to a series of numbered doorways on irregularly sized dwellings on the left: 28, 30, and 32. This is known as the Forgione house, even if the "House" was not a single unit; rather, it consisted of several single-room apartments opening to Vico Storto Valle. The doors are so nondescript, one could easily miss them if it weren't for a prominent plaque and plastic sign on the wall on either side of door number 32. The smaller sign identifies it (in four languages) as the room where Padre Pio was born. In English, it says: "Padre Pio was born here." (The house was originally numbered 27, but later renumbered.) A larger stone plaque to the right of the door, offers a few more details:

> In this little house,
> on May 25, 1887,
> was born Francesco Forgione,
> whom the world knew as
> Padre Pio da Pietrelcina

The door is open. We enter and admire a vintage bedroom on the right, shielded by a protective plexiglass pane. It is strikingly simple. Like the Tower, this room has been outfitted with furnishings from the past. There is a matrimonial size bed with a wrought iron headboard and footboard, a nightstand, some wooden chairs, and an empty shelf recessed in the wall. Against the wall are two wicker baskets and an oil lamp. Affixed to the wall are framed pictures of Zi' Orazio and Zia Giuseppina, Our Lady, and a crucifix. On the floor to the left of the entrance is a trap door. Today it is covered with a glass pane, while the original wood panel has been removed and rests on the wall alongside it. The pane is cloudy making it difficult to discern the wooden stairs that lead to a lower level. Below was once a barn housing Orazio's donkey and (possibly) other farm animals. Since this apartment was hewn into the side of the mountain, the upper floor is accessible via the main door at the street level, while the lower is accessed at the bottom of some stairs to the right.

To the left of the birth house are numbers 30 and 28. Door no. 30 is closed and unidentified, but beyond it is number 28. A plaque in front of this door says that it served as the Forgione kitchen and children's bedroom. We step inside and note that it consists of two rooms. In the first are an original fireplace and old furnishings including kitchen wares, such as terracotta containers, copper pots and pans, and an oil lamp. Beyond the first room is a bedroom where the children (including Francesco) slept, but is now presented as a dining room. It consists of a bench and an old, wooden table with the top propped open. On the right is recessed shelving in the wall replete with old plates, forks, jugs, and other artefacts. The walls are mostly empty with the exception of a black and white photograph of Francesco's mother. A rock in the corner is identified as Padre Pio's pillow.

There are windows at the rear of the rooms that reveal a scenic view of the valley in the distance, including the area of Piana Romana. The thought that young Francesco, his siblings, and parents could gaze out at these beautiful vistas is heartwarming. Though their lives were marked by difficulty and toil, God consoled.

I head back out to the street, step back, and reflect for a moment on the meaning of this site. These rooms are powerful. Within these "houses," Francesco began to have profound spiritual experiences. He had his first ecstasies and diabolical apparitions and became familiar with the Virgin Mary and his Guardian Angel. Don Nicola Caruso, the priest of Pietrelcina, testified as such. He wrote that: "More than once, Francesco told me that when he returned home from school, he found in the doorway a man dressed as a priest who wouldn't let him pass. When Francesco prayed, a barefoot boy would appear and make the sign of the cross and the priest would disappear. Then he would serenely enter."

In front of the birth house are some steps. We climb them (there are precisely twenty), turn left, climb up four more steps, and are now standing in a small square in front of the humble church of Sant'Anna (St. Anne's). It cannot be more than thirty meters (33 yards) from Padre Pio's house.

Sant'Anna is the oldest church in Pietrelcina. It traces its origins to the thirteenth century, but was rebuilt after severe damage from the 1688 earthquake. It held the title as the village's official parish until 1843 when it was transferred to the current parish church – St. Mary of the Angels (then named Santissima Annunziata).

It is immediately clear that this is a special church. Apart from the fact that Padre Pio received his sacraments of Baptism, First Communion, Confirmation, and made regular confession here, there is something unique about it. Tucked away in the farthest corner of the oldest part of Pietrelcina, it has a warm draw to it. The birds tweeting and roosters crowing in the distance only add to the ambiance. It is quiet and prayerful.

The façade is plain white with a nondescript, central door and a smaller one on the right. Above the main door is a stained-glass window depicting a young boy having a vision of Jesus. Ot is a representation of Christ calling Francesco Forgione to the priesthood. Above the window is a simple bell tower. I step inside. The interior is even more pleasant. It consists of two aisles – a main nave on the left and a side aisle on the right. The walls are an off-white color. The low, white, wooden ceiling is coffered and illuminated by a series of chandeliers.

In the main nave, a simple altar railing separates the public space from two altars – a pre-Vatican II altar affixed to the wall, and a modern one set apart. Above the altar is an oil painting depicting what appears to be the translation (flight) of the Holy House of Mary from Nazareth to Loreto. This piques my interest, as I live in Loreto. To the left of the altar is a simple, wooden crucifix, and to the right a resin statue of Padre Pio. On the left wall are stairs leading up to an ancient, wooden pulpit for preaching. On the left side of the nave, aft of the wall pulpit, is a large, recessed space. Within it, behind a protective glass covering, is a baptistery. On the glass are red letters stating, "In this baptismal font, on May 26, 1887, Padre Pio was baptized with the name, Francesco."

In the minor right-hand aisle are two side altars. In the second one is a confessional used by Padre Pio from 1910-16. Just below the wall altar are relics of St. Pius the Martyr. A second-century pope originally buried in the Catacombs of St. Priscilla in Rome, his remains were donated to this church by the Carafa feudal lords in 1801. As I begin walking back outside, my interest is piqued by a wooden board. It is filled with small plates listing the names of American donors who helped restore the church in 1981. I am delighted that Padre Pio is so beloved in my home country.

Back outside, to the right of the church is a low wall. Beneath it is a terrace, or belvedere, offering a relaxing view of the countryside. The vistas – mostly farmland and hills in the distance – are wonderful. It is like a window thrown open to an enchanting horizon. It is not difficult to imagine Francesco Forgione or a young Padre Pio, sitting on this wall gazing out at the countryside, reflecting and meditating. He may have been here when he conceptualized the following words, written in one of his letters and now inscribed on the wall facing the church: "The sun rises and it becomes day and the soul opens up to the sun. But when it passes and shadows come, it forgets, and the Lord takes away even the memory of the consolation it had so that the shadows might become perfect. Expand your soul before this divine sun and do not fear its fiery rays; otherwise, the cocoon will not open up and the well-formed butterfly will not come out." (*Letters* III, no. 21)

I step back and thank God for humble, devotional churches like Sant'Anna. It's as if God gives us churches like this where we can come and meet him in solitude. On the other hand, there are the larger churches. The Baroque parish of St. Mary of the Angels in the center of Pietrelcina is more like an apostolic or evangelical church. Here we listen; there we speak. Here we internalize; there we proclaim. What a beautiful dichotomy.

Continuing in the footsteps of Padre Pio through the old district, in less than fifty meters, we arrive at the "maternal house." A sign posted next to the door identifies it as the home where Padre Pio's mother, Zi' Giuseppa, was born and grew up. We step inside and see a fireplace on the immediate right. To the left is a sitting room with an old table, chest, jugs, cooking ware, pots, and wicker baskets. Just beyond the fireplace is another room with more jugs, wares, and baskets. All are protected with plexiglass.

Immediately above the maternal house is the house of Padre Pio's brother, Michele. Sometimes referred to as the "house of the priest," Padre Pio lived here from 1912-16 after he was ordained. This is the largest of the houses. Like the Tower, it is accessed via a staircase with tall, stone steps. Once inside, on the immediate left is a bedroom identified as that of Mary Pyle, the well-to-do American convert and benefactress of Padre Pio. She lived here from 1941-43. Padre Pio's room is straight ahead, beyond the fireplace. Like his rooms elsewhere, this one, too, is simple. Furnishings consist of a bed, nightstand, water basin, and pictures on the wall, including one of Padre Pio and his brother, Michele.

As we leave Michele's house, our journey takes us back in the same direction from whence we began. The itinerary has taken us around a loop through the old Castle district. There is one way in and out through the compact, old center of Pietrelcina. There cannot be more than fifty abodes in the entirety of this area. It is quaint and simple.

When Padre Pio left Pietrelcina for Foggia on February 17, 1916, he never returned. Yet, he remained forever wistful of his home town. He never forgot his beloved streets, churches, monuments, and especially the faces of the people. He used to say that he remembered "every stone of Pietrelcina." Whenever his townspeople came to San Giovanni Rotondo, his face would radiate in delight. He once wrote to his brother, saying, "I gave value to San Giovanni [Rotondo] during my lifetime; I will give value to Pietrelcina after my death."

As Padre Pio was called elsewhere, it is time for us to leave Pietrelcina. However, we will return. The most important site here, the Piana Romana, has yet to be visited. But before we venture out to the countryside, there are other sites to discover.

7: In the Footsteps: Morcone, Sant'Elia a Pianisi, Campobasso

Today we venture out to the outlying convents – the minor friaries off the beaten path. (Throughout this book, I use the words, "convent" and "friary" interchangeably). In these convents, Padre Pio lived for short periods during formation before arriving permanently in San Giovanni Rotondo. Today we will visit the sites where he lived as a novice and student, Morcone and Sant'Elia a Pianisi, followed by a nearby mountain sanctuary, in Campobasso, where he lived briefly on two separate occasions.

We recall that the fifteen-year-old boy, Francesco Forgione, left his native Pietrelcina for the novitiate in Morcone. While young Francesco traveled by train accompanied by his teacher and parish priest, we will travel by automobile. For navigation, I will use my GPS and Google Maps application in my cellphone. My GPS is programmed to take us on the fastest route. Thus, if it makes for a more efficient trip time, it will take us on wayside country roads and even occasional dirt roads known as *contrade*. Furthermore, the roads between Pietrelcina and Morcone – as elsewhere in this region – are not straight. The territory is too hilly and underdeveloped to warrant a straight highway here. Unlike Northern Italy where the economy is thoroughly industrialized, the South is still agricultural. Nonetheless, I am grateful that our route will offer a more genuine experience out in the countryside on simple roads and allow us to experience the land the way Padre Pio did.

As we set out, the app directs us through only one town just outside of Pietrelcina, Fragnete Monforte. Other than that, there is little between the native town of Padre Pio and Morcone other than clusters of farmhouses, wayside business establishments, and vast tracts of farmland. This time of year, early October, the earth has recently been turned over after the summer harvest. It is a refreshing drive out here in God's creation. This land seems imbued with the presence of Padre Pio.

Occasionally, we pass some old country houses with penned farm animals. I want to stop and take a closer look at the donkeys, ducks, and sheep, but there is no time. It is not difficult to imagine shepherds and peasants from a bygone era walking or traveling in carriages pulled by donkeys or oxen along these dirt roads… or a friar on the *questua*. I begin to feel nostalgic. To my delight, just around a bend, a woman riding a horse on the side of the road passes in the opposite direction. I smile. It seems perfectly apropos.

On the other hand, I am reminded that we are in the twenty-first century by the omnipresent windmills, properly known as wind turbines. Though windmills have been used for at least a millennium up and down this peninsula to grind grains, these sleek, ultra-modern turbines generate remarkable amounts of renewable energy. Made of composite material, they are highly efficient harnessers of wind in this hilly region. On the ridges in the distance, there are dozens of them forming veritable wind farms. As we drive by one at close distance, the sheer size is remarkable. The tower must be at least 300 feet high, each of its three propellers half that. (In fact, I look up the numbers later and discover that the rotor diameter is twice the length of an Airbus 380 wingspan!)

After about thirty minutes of winding about, I see a hill town in front of me. It is Morcone. Like so many other ancient towns in the region (and Italy), it is perched on the side of a mountain. I'm relieved we have arrived, as I am beginning to feel the first pangs of carsickness due to the excessively curvy route. As we approach the outer limits of town, I look up and realize just how steep Morcone is. Fortunately, the Capuchin friary and church are located at the bottom of the hill, just above the plains. I have no interest in driving or walking up that slope. I follow the signs to *"Convento cappuccino"* and soon turn left onto a charming driveway, made of white travertine stone pavers, and pull into a parking lot in an inviting square.

Though the church and friary are now located in a busy, suburb in lower Morcone, I am confident that not too many decades ago, the Capuchins were all alone out here. As hermits, the Capuchins carefully selected the locations for their convents in areas well away from the city centers. They tended to be about five kilometers (3 mi) from town. (As an aside, this is one way to distinguish the Capuchin, Conventual, and Observant Franciscan branches: the Capuchin churches are always small and well outside the city centers, the Conventual churches are large and inside the city walls, and the Observants [OFM] are somewhere in between.)

I get out of my car and take my first look at the church and convent of Morcone. The complex is lovely. I walk toward the church and admire a very old cross close to the entrance. The church is constructed of hewn stone with a small bell tower centered above the main door. The convent, stuccoed and painted a lovely cream color, extends to the right. I notice that the outer door to the convent is open. That is a good sign. Hopefully, someone will be available to show me around.

A plaque fixed to the façade briefly describes the history of the church and convent. It says it is dedicated to Sts. Philip and James and was built in 1500 as a single chapel. In 1603, the marquise of Morcone, a noblewoman named Delponte, enlarged it creating the Capuchin church and convent that has served as a novitiate from the beginning. Another sign in front of the door to the friary says that Padre Pio lived here and visitors can see the cell where he lived, the common fireplace room, the refectory, museum, choir, and gardens. Excellent. I'll ring the bell shortly, but first I will enter the church.

I enter and am struck by a truly gracious interior. The church is divided into two aisles: the main nave to the right and a minor aisle to the left. It has been renovated recently and has an inviting atmosphere. On the right side are statues of saints in niches, while behind the main altar is a statue of Mary flanked by St. Joseph and St. John. In the nave are more statues and niches: St. Anthony of Padua, an unidentified Capuchin saint, St. Francis of Assisi, and Our Lady. I sit on one of the wooden benches and take it in. At the rear of the church is the choir on high. This is where the friars prayed and, I'm assuming, still do.

I exit the church and step over to the convent door adjacent to the church. As I do, I make a heartfelt prayer. These types of visits are hit-miss. Though the sign by the door says visits are available from 9:00-12:00, then from 3:00-6:00 (the three-hour period for midday prayer, lunch, and rest is still observed in these parts), the reality is that inside-the-convent visits are dependent on whether or not there happens to be a friar or someone available to show visitors around. Religious communities are much smaller than they used to be, and the friars who remain tend to be more elderly and busier than ever.

Indeed, when I ring the bell (I have a choice between an old rope that pulls a bell inside the cloister or an intercom – I opt for the modern choice), a woman answers and after I ask if I can see the friary, she says that no friars are available. However, she quickly changes her mind and says that someone will be right out. In Southern Italy, "be right out" is relative. In fact, after five or six minutes, no one comes. I ring again. This time a man answers and assures me that he is coming.

In another five minutes, an elderly friar opens the door and greets me. I identify myself as an American, a Third Order Franciscan, and a devotee of Padre Pio and ask if I can see Padre Pio's cell. (I don't want to push it.) He asks me if I just want to see the cell, or all of it including the fireplace room, refectory, museum, choir, and gardens.

"If it's not too much trouble, all of it." What a treat, I think to myself.

The friar introduces himself as Fra' Donato Ramolo from Limosanto, near Campobasso. Over the next forty-five minutes, I am blessed with a personalized visit of the convent interspersed with personal storytelling. I learn that Fra' Donato recently celebrated his golden jubilee (fifty years) in religious life and has two (birth) brothers who are also Capuchin friars in this Province. While Brother

Donato was never ordained, his siblings were. One was even ordained a bishop and served in the missions in North Africa.

Brother Donato begins the visit in the foyer by narrating the history of the Capuchin friary and church. He says that the marquise (the noblewoman of Morcone), Delponte, went to Spain on a pilgrimage in the sixteenth century and made a vow to St. Francis that if she returned safely, she would build a Franciscan church. In 1603, she came back and honored her vow. She contacted the Capuchin Provincial Minister and financed the construction of the convent.

He points to a wall painting in the foyer. In the center is a boy arriving through the same door I just entered, while a bearded friar greets him. To the left is a field with a small farmhouse and sheep, and to the right is a mountain with footsteps leading to the summit covered by the sun. He explains that the boy is the young Francesco Forgione, the friar is Fra' Camillo of Sant'Elia a Pianisi, and the mountain represents the highest spiritual perfection.

However, he adds that the friary has been altered. The original door to the friary was to the left of the church, while the convent wall enclosed this door. We enter the cloister and he shows me a black and white photograph of the convent and church from a century earlier.

Then Fra' Donato shows me a striking black and white photograph immediately on the wall to the left. It is Fra' Camillo himself. He is a handsome man with a full mantle and graying beard. A small plate below the photo says he was born on October 30, 1871 and died on January 26, 1933.

As I get to know Fra' Donato, I realize he is a wealth of experience and insight into the Capuchin Order in this region. I ask him if he ever met Padre Pio, to which he responds that he confessed to him several times. His novitiate did not take place here in Morcone. Instead, he and his confreres were sent up to the region of Veneto in Northern Italy. He said that in the early '60s, there was an attempt to dismantle the Capuchin Province of Sant'Angelo and Foggia. It was an attempt on behalf of the religious authorities to diminish the "cult of Padre Pio." In fact, when he and the other students met *il Padre* (the Father – the way everyone refers to Padre Pio around here), he wept and asked the students for forgiveness. He said they were being sent away because of him. How many persecutions that man endured.

We walk around the cloister and look at pictures on the wall. There is one listing all the guardians (superiors) of the community of Morcone. Curiously, there is no one listed when Padre Pio arrived here on January 6, 1903. The previous superior was Padre Raffaele da Firenze (May 1901), while from April 1903-April 1906, Padre Francesco Maria da Sant'Elia a Pianisi was superior. We then come to an aerial picture of the Capuchin convent and church from 1908.

My initial hunch is grounded. There was nothing surrounding the Capuchin complex of Morcone but farmland. I mention this to Fra' Donato, and he says that most of the actual buildings around the convent were built in the 1960s and '70s.

"Here in the convent of Morcone, our Province once had the novitiate. Many holy friars did their novitiate here, not just Padre Pio. Venerable Raffaele da Sant'Elia a Pianisi was here, so was Servant of God, Modestino da Pietrelcina. The novitiate in the Capuchin Order is a period of intense retreat or withdrawal (Ita: *ritiro*) from the world. When Fra' Pio was here, there was nothing else out here. It was a hermitage." While I understand progress and that the world changes, I feel a touch of nostalgia. It doesn't seem right that the Capuchin hermitage was engulfed by modernity.

Brother Donato now takes me into what he refers to as the *stanza del fuoco* (the fireplace room). Furnished with artefacts and wares from Padre Pio's era, it reminds me of a movie set. Fra' Donato takes the time to describe every piece. There are objects one would expect to find around an old hearth: thongs, cast iron pots and skillets, and billows. Then there is farm equipment including horseshoes, sheep shears, a hatchet and axe, scythes, hammers, saws, cowbells, and bridles. There are grinding cans for barley beans (which makes a type of decaf coffee), an old-fashioned iron (it has a hollowed space for hot coals), oil lamps and lanterns, skeleton keys, canes, and a walking stick. Fra' Donato points downward and says that this room boasts the original stone flooring, while it has been redone elsewhere in the cloister.

He then points to a brazier. He says that there was no heat anywhere in the convent until the 1980s or so. Prior to that time, the only warm room (during the winter) was this one, the fireplace room.

"Francesco Forgione arrived here on January 6. The first thing Fra' Camillo did was take him here to warm up."

During the cold months, he continues, Capuchin friars throughout the Province (and elsewhere) would gather together by the fire after dinner to warm up before going up to their cells. The elderly and sick friars were permitted to bring a *braciere* (brazier) – a covered metal pan filled with hot coals – to their cells. I tell him that I once thought Southern Italy was warm… that is, until I spent a few winters in my wife's hometown in Puglia. He nods and adds that most of Italy is temperate. The farther one goes inland, and towards the Apennine Mountains, the colder it gets – even in the South.

"It doesn't snow here every season, but we do get a good snowfall every few years." He tells me to remind him to show me the picture in the courtyard of the convent with snow on it.

I ask about the rule regarding footwear. He says that sandals without socks (which is the technical definition of "discalced," or barefoot) was the norm, though elderly and sick friars were permitted to wear socks. He gestures down toward the socks beneath his sandals and states that he is in latter condition. As a septuagenarian, he is not considered elderly. But he has been receiving chemotherapy treatments for the past four years for a "cancer of the blood; that is, leukemia." I tell him I am truly sorry and will remember him in prayer in each site I visit.

"May it be the will of God," he responds with serenity and a smile. I cannot help but smile back.

We make our way around the cloister to the museum. Br. Donato flips on a light switch revealing a rich array of liturgical vestments and vessels. Two walls boast well-illuminated, ceiling-high displays consisting of patens, chalices, a missal and a lectionary, an episcopal miter, stoles, an alb, a habit, a chasuble, and several reliquaries.

"This was all used by Padre Pio… except for the miter," says Brother Donato.

My attention is drawn to a collection of knotted cords and chains. These are the notorious "disciplines." I inquire about them.

"The novices would use these on their bare backs. On Wednesdays and Fridays, they would go into the church, sing the *Miserere*, and imitate the scourging of Jesus on the pillar."

Then, he pauses and becomes pensive for a moment.

"The 'disciplines' are often misunderstood. The practice has to be taken in context," he says.

His demeanor has now changed, and he has become serious. I recognize that he is about to tell me something important.

"This is the life of the Capuchin Order: seeking to imitate Christ Crucified. We seek to live out a close connection to Christ on the cross — to understand what Jesus did for us. The disciplines were a form of meditation, a way to seek conformity to Christ Crucified. It was not a punishment, nor really a type of penance. It was a meditation." I listen intently.

"Punishments took other forms. For example, consider if a novice did something like accidentally break a vase. The broken vase would have been tied around the novice's shoulders for a period of time. Or perhaps they would be ordered to kneel in front of everyone in the refectory and ask forgiveness." I listen as he speaks.

"Another part of their life was silence. The friars always looked at the ground. They never spoke to the novice master or superior without being addressed first. If they needed something, they would go to the door of the novice master, kneel, knock, and say a Hail Mary. If the novice master responded by repeating the Hail Mary, they could enter."

"While these things seem anachronistic today, it is important to understand that life was severe also in the families. Children were disciplined by their parents in a way that might be considered abusive today. Life was different then." I nod my head.

"Even Padre Pio practiced the disciplines before entering the novitiate. He was a child already meditating on the life of Christ in such a way with a cord with which he flagellated his back. It upset his mother, but she never told him to stop the practice."

I ask Fra' Donato if the friars still practice the disciplines, to which he responds matter-of-factly that they do not.

"We stopped after the reforms back in the 1970s or so. Life is very different today – both inside and outside the convent. We can devote our lives to Christ Crucified in other ways."

Next, we enter the old refectory, which is now used as a meeting room. On the wall is a sign saying: "Fra' Pio the novice, of little appetite, sometimes was embarrassed in the refectory, because he had to justify to the novice master and the guardian if he wished to leave food, but the superiors were understanding and they left him in peace, giving him a dispensation before the entire fraternity." Another plaque on the wall recounts other anecdotes about Padre Pio and his obedience as a novice.

We start up the stairs. Halfway up, as the stairs turn ninety degrees to the right, Fra' Donato stops to catch his breath. He uses the pause to point out a painting of Mary. He says that just as all families have a mother of the house, who is the point of reference in the family, the friars have Our Lady. She is the mother of this house for the novices, as well as for the professed friars.

He points to a phrase beneath the painting: *"NE TRANSEAS CAVE NISI PRIUS DIXERIS: 'AVE.'"* As I attempt to put my rudimentary Latin skills to work and wonder if the first verb is in the subjunctive or indicative mood, my guide tells me it is an old Capuchin tradition in which friars were admonished to say a Hail Mary as they went up or down the stairs. He translates for me: "Beware not to pass without first saying an Ave."

He points to a framed short story next to the image of Mary titled, "From the Traditions of the Convent." He summarizes it. Well before the era of Fra' Pio, a novice decided to leave the convent in the middle of the night. As he was descending the staircase, he paused to say his Hail Mary. To his astonishment, the image of Mary spoke to him saying that if he "returned to the world, he would go to hell." He went back up to his cell and remained in the order until his death many decades later.

As we arrive at the top of the stairs, there is a tiny wooden box attached to the wall with a numbered wall chart above it. The box is full of thumb-size chips with numbers on each side. He picks one out, checks the number, then runs his hand along the chart until he finds the corresponding number. It says to pray for souls in purgatory who suffered from the vice of avarice. I pick a number out. Thirty-nine. It says to pray for souls in purgatory who prayed inattentively. I say my prayer silently – secretly hoping that some of the grace against this particular vice will rub off on me, even though I know it doesn't work that way.

The first hallway at the top up the stairs was for the professed friars, says Fra' Donato, while the novices' cells were along another corridor. As we walk in that direction, he adds that there were actually two hallways for the novices. As a way of teaching poverty, the superior did not want them to get too attached to one location, so he moved them after six months. For this reason, Padre Pio had two rooms here in Morcone.

We come to cell no. 28. A small plaque next to it identifies it as that of Padre Pio. Another sign explains that this cell was confirmed as belonging to Padre Pio due to his own words. Over the years, people asked Padre Pio where he stayed in the various convents, and he always remembered the number of each one.

Just above the door is a quote from Scripture. (There is a different verse above every cell.) This one says, "For you have died, and your life is hidden with Christ in God" (Colossians 3:3). It seems apropos to the life of Padre Pio.

We step inside. Like the houses in Pietrelcina, this cell has been retrofitted with vintage furnishings. There is a small, made-up bed, a wooden chair and table with some devotional books, and a cross. I look out the small window and an enamored by the view of the mountains in the background.

Fra' Donato pushes on the top of the mattress so I can see how firm it is. He tells me it is filled with corn husks, just as in Padre Pio's era. Following his lead, I push down on it, too. It feels lumpy. He lifts up the mattress and shows me the metal plank the mattress rests on. It must have been very uncomfortable to sleep on. On the pillow is a simple wooden cross, which the novices placed on their chest when they slept. In the corner, within a stand-up display case, is a night habit worn by the Capuchins when they slept. It looks just like Fra' Donato's habit, except it has no hood or cincture. He says that the habit identifies one's belonging to the Capuchin Order.

"Back in the beginning, early on, St. Francis himself would give the habit to young men asking to follow him. There was no novitiate, or period of formation, then. They only had to give away everything they owned to enter. Then they would live the life. If they discovered the Franciscan life was not for them, they would give the habit back and go back to their old lives. Conversely, if they did something scandalous, they would be deprived of the habit and forced out. The habit represented the order. The friars never took it off, not even when they slept."

In the corner is a porcelain pitcher atop a wash basin. At night, the friars would fill their pitchers with water from the well and bring it up to their rooms to use for washing. I mention that I read that the water sometimes froze in the winter. Fra' Donato says he heard that, too, but he did not experience it firsthand since he did not live here as a novice. He came here only after central heat had been installed. He points to a contemporary wall radiator and adds that the entire convent was renovated according to legal norms back in the 1980s or so.

On the wall is an authentic framed letter written by Padre Pio's own hand. His penmanship is gorgeous. Next to it is a shorter handwritten letter in the same hand. It is his request to be admitted to profession. Another sign on the wall says that Padre Pio came back to Morcone more than once after his novitiate, especially since the convent was near Pietrelcina. He returned on July 18, 1909 to be ordained to the diaconate; on July 21, 1910, to learn the rites of the Mass before ordination; and in July, 1914, after being ordered by the provincial to return to the order, but was forced to return home immediately thereafter for health reasons.

We make our way to another corridor and Fra' Donato shows me the other room Padre Pio occupied: cell no. 18. The verse above the door says: "The cross is always ready and awaits you everywhere."

Donato says this is not scriptural, but is taken from the classic spiritual treatise, *Imitation of Christ*, by Thomas à Kempis. Once again, Pio's verse seems fitting. Fra' Donato says that this cell is not open to the public and is currently occupied by one of the professed friars in residence.

Just beyond the second novice's corridor and Padre Pio's cell is the choir. It is located on high, over the external door at the rear of the church. Fra' Donato points to some benches against the wall and says that the professed friars used to sit here. The novices did not have seats. Instead, they stood or knelt. The once empty area has now been filled with movable benches.

He says that as in all their Capuchin churches in the Province, as well as throughout Southern Italy, the choirs are always in the back of the church, above the main entrance. It is typical of Capuchin convents in Southern Italy. Elsewhere in Italy, as in Camerino – where the order was founded – the choirs are to the side of the church. What is similar, however, is that they are made of wood – poor materials.

In the center of the choir is a prominent, wooden lectern set on a swivel. On one side rests a hefty, leatherbound psalter, and a book of Gregorian chant on the other. In the old days, friars did not have their own private breviaries. Instead, they read from the central psalter. A novice pulled leather straps moving the lantern-illuminated lectern back and forth while each side prayed, alternating in chant.

Brother Donato leads me to the far side of the choir. On the floor is something like a trap door opening to a very steep staircase. The novices would go down here to receive communion in the rear of the church below. During their novitiate, they were seen by practically no one. It was essentially a monastic experience. They only left the convent twice during the entire one-year period: once to go into Morcone to visit a sanctuary, and later to a different village to visit another shrine. This is the reason no one in Morcone could recall young Pio when he was a novice. They never saw him.

Lastly, he points to a wooden crucifix just behind the lectern. Christ is dying in agony.

"All our convents have a crucifix similar to this one. Christ Crucified is the point of reference in our lives. Always Christ crucified. Even if our life is different than in the past, he remains at the center." He makes the sign of the cross, as we head back down to the cloister.

Finally, Fra' Donato takes me outside to the immaculate grounds behind the convent. I am stunned by a massive, immaculate garden. Fra' Donato says it's about two hectares (5 acres) and has 130 olive trees, some fig trees, a small vineyard. However, in the past it was all farmland worked by the novices. Farm work was an important part of their activities, he adds.

Before we say goodbye, Brother Donato brings me into his work room where he shows me a series of crafts made by his own hand. He is an expert in wood inlay. Many of his works have an African motif, and I learn that like his brother, the bishop, he was a missioner in Ethiopia and North Africa for many decades. The Africans taught him the trade. His work is gorgeous.

I wish I could spend much more time here in Morcone. The gardens alone merit a half day. Unfortunately, we have to leave. We need to be at our next stop no later than 11:30. Though the Franciscans have a saying: "God made time, the devil made haste," the reality is that everything shuts down after noon and doesn't open until early afternoon. I do not want to miss our next visit.

I return to my car and enter Sant'Elia a Pianisi in my GPS. It says it will take fifty-three minutes. I look at my watch. Eleven o'clock. That's cutting it short. If I channel my inner Schumacher, I may be able to shave a few minutes off the trip. While my methane-powered Opel Zafira is no Ferrari, if I step on it, we should be able to make it before closing time.

Once back on the road, as elsewhere, the route consists of a series of provincial roads through the countryside and mountains. The roads are not in good condition. I have to slow down significantly along a few stretches marked by significant cracks, rutting, and depressions. On two occasions, a traffic signal has been installed to separate two lanes of traffic into one because one side of the road has been completely washed out in an apparent mudslide.

After a steep climb with some serious switchbacks, we reach the pass at a village called Pietracatella. It is little more than a few houses built around a ruined fortress. Then we continue for another eight kilometers (5 mi) along a ridge to Sant'Elia. As we approach our destination (with a close eye on the time), I can't help but wonder how the friars, including Padre Pio, got out here.

No sooner do we arrive within the town limits of Sant'Elia a Pianisi than the Capuchin complex appears on the outskirts of town. I park by a statue of St. Anthony and check the time. Eleven forty-five. Perfect. Since time is of the essence, I go straight to the convent door. We can visit the church next. I ring the intercom.

A woman's voice says, "*Sì?*" I introduce myself just like back in Morcone and ask if I can see Padre Pio's cell. She says that, unfortunately, the friars are out. In my sweetest, most mendicant voice, I explain that I am American, from the Third Order of St. Francis, a devotee of Padre Pio, and have come all the way from Pietrelcina and Morcone… actually, all the way from America… to see the cell of Padre Pio, and *per favore* is there anything that can be done? She tells me to "*aspettà*" (wait). I hold my breath. To my relief, in a few minutes, the door opens. Removing her apron, my interlocutor smiles and says she will show me around.

"Yes!!!" I shout to myself interiorly. Even if I get the abbreviated visit in Sant'Elia a Pianisi, my main goal is to see the cell where Padre Pio had a vision of the black dog and to visit the choir where the first bilocation took place. I'll take what I get.

On our way to the cell, she leads me into a well-illuminated museum with equivalent items on display as elsewhere: liturgical vestments and vessels; relics including a glove, hair, and a scab; and black and white photographs. After a cursory visit, we make our way toward the cell of Padre Pio. Along the corridor is another smaller museum with items from the life of Venerable Raffaele da Sant'Elia a Pianisi. It consists of relics similar to those in the Padre Pio museums – liturgical items and vestments.

As we arrive at Padre Pio's cell, a sign above the door says, "In this cell, Padre Pio da Pietrelcina studied, prayed, exercised in love of God, and struggled against Satan from January, 1904 to October,

1907, and he consecrated himself an exemplary Capuchin with his solemn profession." We step inside. The cell is unusually tiny. Just as in Morcone, it is outfitted with furnishings from the early twentieth century: a narrow bed with a mattress stuffed with corn husks, a terracotta carafe and wash basin, a wooden cross for sleeping, and a simple wooden desk and chair.

I walk over to the window and ask if I can open it. She nods her head. I do so and look outside. It is, indeed, very close to the one next to it, separated by just a few centimeters. I mention that I read that Fra' Pio's cell was close to that of his companion, and they used to pass books to one another. She concurs and adds that his name was Fra' Anastasio. I ask about the dog and where it appeared. She says it came in from the doorway, where she is standing, and jumped through the window, where I am standing. I shudder.

Though I would prefer to spend more time here, my American "I-don't-want-to-burden-you-and-waste-your-time-because-I-know-you're-busy" mentality emerges, and I walk out indicating we can move on. She then leads me back downstairs and shows me into a room where *"Ci incontriamo"* (we meet). She, too, is a Third Order Franciscan. After a brief visit in the courtyard, she says she has to get back to the kitchen. I thank her profusely for her time. She smiles and says it was a pleasure. Her joyful disposition tells me she means it. She points out the direction to the sacristy and tells me I can enter the church from there. After she disappears, I realize I never even asked my kindly guide for her name. Like the friar I met earlier, she, too, has been a blessing.

I enter the church and look around. It is magnificent. Apart from the numerous side altars with statues in niches, there is a striking work of art behind the main altar. It consists of a massive wooden structure with eight panel paintings – five on the bottom, three on the top. I suppose it would be considered a *pala d'altare* (the term translates poorly into English as simply "altarpiece"), that is, a large, one-, three-, or five-panel decorative backdrop set over and above altars. But this piece is so large, it might qualify as a *retablo* (retable), common in churches throughout Spain.

At this point, a friar arrives in the sacristy. I approach him and begin to introduce myself, but he says that Teresa already told him I was here. He asks if I have seen everything inside the convent to my satisfaction, to which I assure him I have. He takes time to point out a few things in the church, including the relics of Venerable Raffaele da Sant'Elia a Pianisi. He says he died three years before Padre Pio came here, that is, two years before he entered the novitiate in Morcone. As such, they never met. From the time of his death, Raffaele's body was buried in the cemetery here. In 1936, they moved his skull into the church and placed it in a niche on the wall to the left of the main altar. In 2017, just as he was going to be declared venerable, it was moved farther back into a more prominent niche. It is surrounded by an attractive painting depicting scenes from his life.

After the friar returns into the convent, I spend some quiet time in prayer. As I do, I recall the episode in which Padre Pio experienced his first bilocation. It took place in the choir when he was praying with Brother Anastasio. I realize that Teresa did not bring me into the choir, so I turn around and look up. There he had a vision of the birth of his spiritual daughter, Giovanna Rizzani, while her father died.

Once again, I don't want to leave, but we must. There just isn't enough time. I return to my car and enter Campobasso into the GPS. The Capuchins have two communities there. The more important one is in the center of town and served as a seminary in the past. But my goal is the other one – the one on top of the mountain: the Sanctuary of our Lady of the Mount. Though this was not a significant convent in the life of Padre Pio, it is close to Sant'Elia and logistically feasible for today's excursion. I climb into my car and we depart.

Campobasso is the capital city of the region of Molise. It is located in the high basin of the Biferno River, surrounded by the Sannio and Matese mountains. I forgot that earlier today, at some point, we had crossed the border between the regions of Campania and Molise. Not long after we leave the village of Sant'Elia, I am pleasantly surprised to merge onto a new highway. The entire trip is straight and takes only about twenty minutes.

After a short lunch break, I load the Capuchin sanctuary into my GPS. I discover that my destination is the large castle and church at the top of a high mountain known as Monforte that I had been seeing for many kilometers as we approached Campobasso. After a number of hairpin turns, and mistaking two Romanesque-era churches dedicated to St. Bartholomew and St. George for my destination, we continue to the top of the mountain. After two more switchbacks, we arrive at a parking lot between a castle and a large Romanesque church. We must be in the right place, because there is a large bronze statue of Padre Pio to the left of the façade. This is the *Santuario della Madonna del Monte* (Sanctuary of Our Lady of the Mount).

A commemorative signpost to the right of the church recounts the story of Fra' Pio and his two stays here. It says that in 1905, as a young newly professed friar, he arrived with other friars from Sant'Elia a Pianisi. That same year, the church had been returned to the custody of the Capuchins of this Province after the decree of the Suppression of the Catholic Church was mitigated. Fra' Pio came with other students to assist in liturgical services for the inauguration. Later, in 1909, he returned for sanitary reasons. He was hoping the healthy mountain air would aid his lungs. He stayed in a room to the right of the church.

I enter the church. Though the façade is clearly Romanesque, the interior is not. It was recently renovated and decorated with contemporary art. I move over to the room on the right that once hosted the saint. Now converted into a chapel, it is more like a museum. Behind some glass encasements are liturgical vestments worn by Padre Pio, and on the walls are black and white pictures of Padre Pio's parents and the ancient church of San Giovanni Rotondo in the early twentieth century.

Above the altar is a painting dated 1972. On the right side, Padre Pio is kneeling with an angel behind him, gazing at Mary, who is standing on the left side. In the middle, Christ lumbers up a mountain carrying a weighty cross. Behind Padre Pio is an open window revealing the castle of Monforte; the actual one is a few meters away. The castle and mountains represent the virtue of fortitude.

As I return to my car and we begin descending the mountain making our way back to Pietrelcina, I see a theme: mountains. Although it seems Padre Pio was sent to the higher altitudes to breathe in the salutary air hoping it would bring respite to his lungs, there is something else about the mountaintops. They are prophetic. From the prophets of the Old Testament – God spoke to Moses on Mt. Sinai and Elijah on Mt. Carmel – to Christ in the New Testament – Jesus was transfigured on Mt. Tabor – to the saints – even St. Francis climbed Mt. Laverna where he received the stigmata, God revealed himself from on high. They climbed the mountains to hear the voice of God. And so did Padre Pio.

8: In the Footsteps: Gesualdo and Benevento

Today's visits involve some of the minor sites in the footsteps of Padre Pio. In the morning, we will visit two convents, Gesualdo and Montefusco, where Padre Pio lived for brief periods and which underwent significant alterations after an earthquake in 1980. Around noontime, we will go to the city of Benevento with the hopes that the cathedral where Padre Pio was ordained is open. As most churches close during the midday lunch and rest period, it may not be possible to visit. Further, the actual chapel where Padre Pio's ordination took place no longer exists, as the entire cathedral was bombed to the ground in World War II.

I set my GPS for Gesualdo. As we depart Pietrelcina to the south, my route takes me on a well-groomed highway in the direction of Avellino. At Benevento, my GPS tells me to turn east and eventually merge onto the autostrada (motorway) toward Bari. I like this. The private autostrada is the pinnacle of highway driving in Italy. The motorways are fast, straight, and efficient. It's nice to be off the tortuous country roads for a change. On the other hand, views of the landscape are limited due to the high speeds, in addition to the steady autumnal rain falling (and forecast for the entire day) rendering visibility nonexistent.

After about ten minutes, my GPS tells me to exit at Grottaminarda and head south past Carpignano to Gesualdo. As we enter the outskirts of the village, I am pleased to see the characteristic red sign denoting Gesualdo as one of the "*Borghi più Belli d'Italia*" (Loveliest Villages of Italy). A national designation, it means that the town boasts quality heritage in terms of cultural activities and architectural and artistic attractions. Unfortunately, I cannot see anything due to heavy fog.

As we get closer to the town, we start to climb. As elsewhere, Gesualdo is located on a hill. I look at my external temperature gauge, which has suddenly dropped from 15.5 degrees Celsius back on the motorway to 13 here (56 to 61 Fahrenheit). Due to Italian topography, the country is dotted with microclimates. Weather patterns are not homogenous even within short distances.

The GPS takes us to Viale Cappuccino (Capuchin Avenue), which is a long, narrow street lined with contemporary apartments. At the end of the road sits the church and convent. Again, it is clear that the Capuchin complex – now surrounded by modern life – was once isolated out here.

I park in the square in front of the church and look up at the simple, white frontage and the convent. On the right side of the façade is a large banner depicting a prominent face of Padre Pio with no associated text. To the right is a bronze statue of our saint. I walk toward the church and note a stone plaque near the façade. It says:

> In this Convent of the Capuchins
> among study and celestial visions
> Padre Pio
> consumed by the Love of God and of his brothers
> lived here in the year of the Lord 1909
> his Confreres [hereby commemorate him] in perpetual memory
> on the Centenary of his residence
> Gesualdo, 2009

I step inside the church and look around. It is comprised of a single aisle with one recessed side altar on the left and two on the right. The right-side niches are fitted with statues of an unidentified Capuchin saint and St. Anthony of Padua. On the left, the altar is decorated with a statue of Mary and the Christ child and a large San

Damiano crucifix. Above the main altar is a grandiose oil painting on canvas depicting numerous saints and other personages. I pick out Sts. Catherine of Siena and Dominic, as well as some nobility and a cardinal on the bottom. I wonder how two Dominican saints found their way into this Franciscan church. On either side of the main altar are statues of Padre Pio and St. Michael the Archangel.

Unlike the other churches I have visited, the interior is dark. There is little natural light, limited by small windows near the ceiling beneath the cross vaults. I don't like to admit it, but this church does not have the same feel as the others. I look to the back to verify that the choir is above the rear of the church. It is. This is still a Capuchin church.

I head back outside and over to the friary and ring the bell. To my delight, an elderly male voice responds quickly. I ask him if I can see Padre Pio's cell to which he says he'll be right out. In less than two minutes, a gray-bearded friar with a brown zucchetto (skullcap) on his head opens the door and smiles. He looks over my shoulder and asks if there's anyone else.

"Just me."

He says that's okay and he'll show me around anyway.

I introduce myself and tell him briefly why I'm here. H says his name is Padre Emidio Cappabianca da Macchia Valfortore. Sensing my confusion at his native town, he says it's a small village near Campobasso, and no one has ever heard of it.

We enter the church and after turning on the lights, Padre Emidio begins recounting the history of the Capuchins here in Gesualdo. It is clear from the outset that Padre Emidio is erudite. He mixes some French and German (which I do not know) into his Italian spiel and takes a stab at English. He attempts to say "Good morning" and "Good night" in what comes across as more Germanic than Anglo. He asks for forgiveness and clarifies that he tried to learn English in school, but it didn't go well, so he stuck with the other languages. Padre Emidio adds that he also reads Latin and Greek, as he was trained to teach the friars of the Province.

I learn that the church and convent have been part of the Capuchin Order since the sixteenth century, though the complex was originally part of the Naples Province. After the Suppression, it sat empty for decades, until the early 1900s when it was returned to the order, this time to their Province, Sant'Angelo and Foggia. This was due to the efforts of a saintly friar named Padre Pio da Benevento. He traveled about on foot with the mission to reclaim suppressed Capuchin friaries and churches.

Padre Emidio tells me that he arrived in Gesualdo in 2004 after this church had once again been abandoned. This time, it was due to "*il terremoto*." People from these parts speak of "the earthquake" as people everywhere refer to local tragedies that have been deeply impressed into the collective memory. He is referring to the massive 6.9 quake in 1980 with epicenter in nearby Irpinia that led to 2,500 deaths and 250,000 homeless.

"Everything was destroyed in the village and out here, including the church," said Padre Emidio. Reconstruction in town was slow, so the villagers bought land out here in the "suburbs" and built up the area. Prior to the earthquake, it was rural. As he continues showing me around, he refers constantly to the earthquake and the renovations. The church and convent underwent substantial alterations. Though he doesn't say as much, it's clear the workmanship was shoddy. I soon discover why the church is so dark. The once large, illuminous windows atop both sides of the nave were decreased in size by more than a half.

We return to the cloister and Padre Emidio points out numerous black and white photographs on the wall and tells stories. He points to one in which an elderly Padre Pio is standing in the middle of a crowd of lively, young friars. He points to each one and identifies them.

"Padre Tommaso was the Provincial for years... Padre Nazzario died three years after ordination... Padre Michele just died a few weeks ago... Padre Gabriele went to Africa as a missioner... Padre Vincenzo is in the community of San Giovanni Rotondo, though he's in the infirmary... Padre Raffaele is also in San Giovanni Rotondo and is still active."

Then he points to a smiling, bespectacled friar with black hair and beard standing to the left of Padre Pio. His attention is turned to a peer in front of him with whom he is bantering.

"*Eccomi!*" (There I am!), he says with an air of satisfaction.

"You met Padre Pio?"

"*Certo*" (Sure).

"Did you ever confess to him or have the chance to meet him?"

"I was at his side when he died," he says matter-of-factly as if he had merely served at one of his Masses. What an unexpected encounter, I think to myself. After probing a little more, I soon realize that I am standing in the presence of one of the last living eyewitnesses of St. Padre Pio. I ask him to tell me more.

During the mid-1960s, Padre Emidio was in Rome studying at the Pontifical Gregorian University. During the summers of 1966, '67 and '68, he came down to San Giovanni Rotondo to help out. He had the occasion to confess to Padre Pio, serve him meals, and assist Mass alongside him. He says he is one of the last ones from that class.

We continue around the courtyard and as Padre Emidio talks, I try to deflect the conversation back to Padre Pio and his experiences with him. But first, he shows me a photograph of Fra' Camillo da Sant'Elia a Pianisi. This one is unique. Fra' Camillo is standing, while a young, black-haired and black-bearded Padre Pio is squatted down beneath him caressing a lamb. Padre Pio is wearing his well-known gloves. He tells me that Fra' Camillo died here in this convent and is buried in the cemetery. He was well-loved in the Province due to his role as the "bearded friar" who drew Padre Pio to the order. The two remained fond of one another throughout their lives.

We enter the refectory, but not before stopping a second time and going over some of the same photographs again. Padre Emidio is eighty-four years old. I don't tell him we already looked at these pictures; I actually enjoy hearing about them again. We enter the refectory, which appears as a modern dining room, if not large. Only the floor is original, says Padre Emidio. There is also a rotating wheel in the back, through which the cooks used to pass food. There was little contact with the laity in the past, he says casually.

"Back then, this refectory was full. Now everything is different. We're only two left."

As we walk toward the stairs, he opens the window, looks out, and tries to show me the mountains in the background. Unfortunately, he can't see much due to the rain and fog. He points to the right and says that in the distance is the mountain of Montevergine. He squints his eyes, but concludes it is not visible.

"Padre Pio's mother wanted him to enter the Benedictine monastery up there," he says as he points out into the whiteness. "Our life was very difficult back then. She was worried about his health." I look for myself and am unsure if I see the contours of a mountain or not. I see something… I think… maybe it's a mountain, maybe not. This reminds me of what it's like trying to understand the local dialects down here. Very foggy.

"Francesco Forgione liked our beards," Padre Emidio says as he tussles playfully at his long, gray beard. "He had to be a Capuchin."

We start up the stairs and pass the box with numbered chips and corresponding prayer chart for suffrage. He says that all the Capuchin convents have them. There is also the same picture of Our Lady with the Latin inscription admonishing the friars to not pass by without saying a Hail Mary. At the top of the stairs, I am struck by a modern hallway – more 1980s-style renovations. In this corridor, the doors are spaced out much farther. He says that during the most recent renovation, three cells were merged into one room. The friars' cells now consist of a bedroom, study, and private restroom. He points out where Fra' Camillo's cell was, though today it is a solid wall.

On our way to Padre Pio's cell, we pass through a museum. There are books, vestments, a psalter, and tunics worn by Padre Pio. There is also a unique bronze reliquary in the form of a tree displaying a glove, scab, and hair from Padre Pio. He says that a few decades ago, San Giovanni Rotondo sent out similar relics to all the friaries. This is why the museums and relics are basically the same in all the convents.

Finally, we enter Padre Pio's cell. It is much larger than it was originally due to the renovations. Most of the furnishings are modern, unlike in Morcone and Sant'Elia, with the exception of a handful of artefacts. On the floor by the bed (which has a mattress stuffed with maize husks) is a pair of old slippers, and below the window is the familiar wash basin and pitcher. There is an old desk and chair, which was "brought from a student's cell in Sant'Elia," adds Padre Emidio, though he clarifies that nothing here belonged to Padre Pio, with the exception of some relics in an alcove.

As we're talking about relics, Padre Emidio casually mentions that he used to own a personal collection of relics of Padre Pio: some of his hair, fingernail clippings, and a large scab. However, over the years, he gave most of them away. He still has a tiny bit of his scab left. Fascinated, I inquire about the scab. He says that the day before Padre Pio died, on September 22, he was personally cleaning the saint's hands after Mass, and a little bit of scab flaked off. He collected it and has kept it ever since. I ask if I can see it, and he says yes, but he'll have to find it. He adds that it is well-documented that Padre Pio's wounds had healed the day he died, that is, the next day, to which I comment that he may very well be in possession of the last scab of Padre Pio. Padre Emidio nods his head in agreement.

After the visit to Padre Pio's cell, Padre Emidio begins to say farewell, and I remind him about the relics. He says, "*Ah, sì,*" and we head down a corridor. (We may have already been down this hallway, but I am disoriented by the labyrinthine, post-1980, renovations.) We enter what looks like a study. Padre Emidio opens a drawer and begins to pull out a diverse assortment of items. It consists of: old newspaper articles, magazine clippings, black and white photographs, random sacks of postcards and prayer cards, and yellowed envelopes with his Capuchin provincial letterhead filled with things. He digs around the pile until he retrieves a plastic wrapper with something miniscule inside. He hands it to me.

"Hold it up to the light so you can see it better." I hold the small plastic bag and squint my eyes as I gaze at a pupil-sized, reddish speck. This is the final scab that flaked off Padre Pio's hands just as his hands healed.

"That's all I have left of it," he says. "A few months ago, some friends from Majorca came and I gave part of it to them."

My heartrate begins to increase as I ask (humbly and prayerfully), "What would an American friend have to do to obtain a relic such as this?"

"I'm not sure… Maybe ask around San Giovanni Rotondo or Pietrelcina."

(I believe) sensing my disappointment, he rummages through the pile, pulls out an old envelope, and extracts a gauze-like material spotted with yellow and brown stains.

"You can have this," he says as he hands it to me.

When they exhumed Padre Pio's body, a damp burial cloth was found beneath the remains. I now own a piece of that cloth.

"Since it absorbed the remains of his body, it's considered a first-class relic," he says.

Moved beyond measure and shocked at the unexpected gift, I begin weeping. Padre Emidio then picks up a paper bag and begins filling it up with other items and relics.

"These prayer cards were touched to Pio's body when they opened the tomb," he says as he deposits a couple dozen second-class relics into another sack. For good measure, he throws in a magazine article, an original black and white photograph of Padre Pio, some stickers of his face to put on my windshield, and other common third-class relics – pieces of cloth that have been touched to his tomb. I remain speechless.

After thanking Padre Emidio profusely for everything he has done for me including the personal stories and his time – and especially these precious gifts – we embrace and say *arrivederci*. This is not an *addio* (goodbye); rather, it means "until we see one another again." I am confident we will. I load my bag of relics of Padre Pio into my car and feel so overjoyed, I decide to skip the next stop on my itinerary, Montefusco. I want to savor the moment. I am too full to take in anything else.

As we're driving west in the direction of Benevento along the autostrada, I smile at the ways of God. Instead of a what I believed would be a minor visit to check a site off my list and take a few photographs, I had a personal encounter with someone who witnessed the death of Padre Pio. This visit was the gift of a lifetime. If I went home today, my pilgrimage would have been a success.

As we approach Benevento, I am unsure if I should turn toward Pietrelcina or continue into the city center. I received so much from my visit with Padre Emidio, I do not want to be distracted by anything else. At the last minute, I decide to take the exit to Benevento. There is little to see other than the rebuilt chapel and I can make it quick. This visit really should be a minor one.

I follow the GPS to the cathedral, park, and approach the church from the south side. While viewing the exterior of the side nave from this viewpoint, it is apparent that it is modern. I walk to the front, and look at the façade and bell tower, which appear original; that is, built during the Middle Ages. To my delight, the door is open. Just inside, on the counter-façade is a plaque with the following text (in Italian written in Latinate style):

> This sacrosanct cathedral basilica
> destroyed due to bellicose episodes in September 1943
> modernly resurrected between 1950-1965
> HIS EXCELLENCY MSGR. CARLO MINCHIATTI
> the Metropolitan of Benevento
> Consecrated [it] to the Glory of the Lord
> and entitled it newly
> THE GREAT MOTHER OF GOD ASSUMED IN HEAVEN
> on 18 December of the Marian year 1987
> in renewing the ancient rites
> by the Bishop Davide and the Archbishop Orsini

I look around at the interior, which is lovely. It appears reconstructed in the same Romanesque style according to the original dimensions. In fact, it looks like a traditional, Roman basilica. It consists of a main nave with no transept flanked by two side aisles on either side. There are numerous windows rendering it airy and bright. It boasts a handsome baldachin above the main altar and a large mosaic just over the pulpit.

According to my research, Padre Pio was ordained in a chapel to the left of the main altar. I see a door immediately to the left of the pulpit, but it is locked. On the other side of the altar is an open door leading to an archaeological exhibit. I make my way over there and am delighted to discover that it is staffed by a gentleman seated at a desk talking to two colleagues. I inquire about Padre Pio's ordination and ask where it took place.

"In the Chapel of the Canons. But it's closed and won't reopen until 16:00…" (Italians use the 24-hour clock.) Instead of dismissing me, he pulls a massive key ring out from a desk drawer, selects one of the keys, hands it to one of his associates, and tells her to open the door for me. Delighted at all the doors that are opening to me figuratively and literally today, I inquire about the chapel. He confirms that the entire church was bombed to the ground in World War II, with the exception of the façade and the bell tower. The church was rebuilt as closely as possible to the original specifications.

As my guide and I make our way to the other side of the nave, I ask her if there are any plaques or statues commemorating Padre Pio's ordination here.

"*Sì*," she says as she unlocks the door. As we cross the threshold, she points to a large, bronze statue immediately on the right. A kneeling Padre Pio is being ordained, while a mitered bishop stands above him with his hands on his head. Integrated into the statue is an open book with the words, "SACERDOS ALTER CHRISTUS" (Priest Another Christ) on one "page" and a glass-encased reliquary containing a scab on the other.

At the base of the statue is a plaque saying:

IN THIS SACRED AREA
ON 10 AUGUST 1910
ST. PIO OF PIETRELCINA
RECEIVED PRIESTLY ORDINATION
FROM MSGR. PAOLO SCHINOSI
AUXILIARY ARCHBISHOP OF BENEVENTO

With that, we have completed our itinerary in the footsteps of Padre Pio for the day. And what a day it has been. As we make our way back to my base in Pietrelcina, I think of Scripture: "My head is anointed with oil; my cup overflows" (Psalm 23:5). I will forever remember this day and the generosity shown to me by Padre Emidio Cappabianca da Macchia Valfortore.

9: In the Footsteps: San Marco la Catola, Venafro, Serracapriola

I am grateful for yesterday's light afternoon and plenty of rest. I'll need it. Today we will have a full day visiting three more convents: San Marco la Catola, Venafro, and Serracapriola. It will require traversing the three regions that make up the vast Capuchin Province of Sant'Angelo and Padre Pio: Campania, Puglia, and Campobasso. According to my GPS, we will cover 320 kilometers (200 mi). Though not logistically sound, today's itinerary is the only way I can get to all the sites in my limited time.

I set my initial destination into my GPS, San Marco la Catola, and set out on the sixty-two-kilometer (40-mile) jaunt one hour to the northeast. We head in the direction of Sant'Elia a Pianisi and after about forty-five minutes, turn east on a highway in the valley. Fortunately, most of the route is straight. As elsewhere, the region is rural and agricultural, and I take delight in the surrounding mountains.

When my GPS says we are ten minutes from San Marco la Catola, I pull over and take a closer look at the map. I see that the Capuchin convent is located just to the south of the village and there appear to be two ways to get there. The first involves a tortuous road with numerous switchbacks that leads first into town and then down to the convent. Or, I can continue a few kilometers and opt for a straight road that arrives directly at the convent. I elect for the second option. Straight is better than twisty, I (foolishly) believe.

As we pass the first road up to San Marco la Catola, my GPS goes briefly into rerouting mode and then concludes that the best road is the second one – the straight one that goes directly to the convent. This confirms my decision. In just over one minute, I arrive at the straight road and turn left off the highway. I stop for a moment as I check out this road. Something seems amiss. It is not asphalt; it is concrete. It is also narrow, slightly wider than a driveway. However, it appears recently paved and seems solid. Even though there is a triangular road sign (denoting warning) saying that trucks are prohibited due to an incline greater than 10%, I go. No sooner do I start up than I realize I made a mistake. I soon understand why the other road was curved and this one is straight. It is straight up.

I keep my car in first gear because I cannot accelerate faster than ten kilometers per hour (6 mph). I want to turn back, but I'm committed. The road is so narrow, there is no space to turn around. If someone comes down the hill in the opposite direction, I suppose I'll have to coast backwards until we find a place wide enough to pass one another. This is the steepest road I've ever driven up. If it were wet, I wouldn't have the traction to go anywhere; I'd just spin the wheels.

After a few minutes, I pass a sign saying the road is closed ahead. Good grief. I suppose I can stop there and walk the rest of the way up. Then, after the visit, I can put the car in neutral and coast back down the mountain. At a certain point, the road levels out. Thank goodness… It's much easier to negotiate now. However, as we come around a turn, to my horror, there is a massive pool of rainwater and mud straddling the road ahead. If I slow down, I'll get bogged down. So I accelerate and hold my breath. I hit the puddle at about 20 km/h (12 mph). Mud and water spray in all directions and I cringe as something scrapes the bottom of my car. I make it through, somehow, miraculously, and my muddy tires are able to grip the concrete as the road again continues up at an incline greater than 10%.

Finally, we begin to flank the retaining walls of what I am assuming to be the Capuchin convent on our left. As we emerge at the top of the straight road, I daub the sweat off my forehead, turn left, and enter the convent parking lot. I get out, look at my mud-coated car, shake my head, and resolve to never again take a straight road up a mountain.

I force the arrival at the convent of San Marco la Catola out of my mind, look around, and am immediately pleased I came out here. It's out in the countryside. I am delighted by the sound of roosters crowing and birds tweeting in the vicinity. Urban creep has not enveloped this site, which allows me to personally experience the hermitage aspect that is at the heart of Capuchin life and spirituality. My drive up the steep hillside tells me why it's still isolated: the convent is on the edge of a cliff; there's nowhere to build.

I look up at the church and convent. Both are cream colored with grey trim around the windows and doors. While the other Capuchin churches we have visited are asymmetrical, here there are four windows to the left of the façade and as many to the right. It is pleasant to look upon. I head into the church.

The interior is also warm and welcoming. Unlike Morcone and Sant'Elia, the church consists of a single nave, though there is a wide, recessed chapel on the right. It has a tall ceiling and is bright with two windows on the left letting in an ample amount of light. Above the main altar is a lovely, wooden icon of a crowned Mary and Christ child. I look around at the niches and see the regulars: St. Anthony, St. Francis, and, of course, Padre Pio. On the right, in the pushed out side chapel, is a statue of an obscure Capuchin saint. I look closer and read a metal plate that identifies him as St. Ludwig, a sixteenth-century German saint.

I go back outside to the convent door and ring the bell. A friar opens up and invites me in. After introducing myself and exchanging pleasantries, I realize he is not Italian. His name is Fr. Denis Lobo and he tells me he is from India. Just then, the guardian, who is Italian, hurries by saying he's late for something and tells Fr. Denis to show me around. He accepts his assignment hesitantly and asks my pardon clarifying that he has only been in San Marco la Catola for just five weeks and is not well-versed on the details. I switch to English, which Fr. Denis seems more confident conversing in, and tell him that I really just want to visit the cell and church.

As we make our way upstairs to the cloister, Fr. Denis says that Padre Pio came out here twice, the first time as a student. The convent of Sant'Elia a Pianisi was closed for renovations and he and the other students continued philosophy studies here for thirteen months. Later, he came back in 1918 to meet with Padre Benedetto, the Provincial Minister, who was staying here. As we walk down the corridor, Fr. Denis points out a painting of a full-size Padre Benedetto. A plate next to the door identifies it as the Provincial's cell.

After a few more few steps down the corridor, we arrive at the cell of Padre Pio. A small plaque next to the door says, "In this cell, P. Pio da Pietrelcina, lived as a priest in the year 1918." We enter the room, which is similar to the other cells we have already visited. Next to the wall is a narrow bed with a slight wooden cross atop a cornhusk mattress. Elsewhere there are a wash basin and pitcher, an old chair, and a nightstand. In the wall at the foot of the bed are a recessed alcove with photographs of Padre Pio's parents, two oil lamps, and a candle.

The right-hand wall of the cell has a door-sized opening in it leading to an adjacent room, which has been converted into a museum. It consists of a full wall encasement displaying some relics and accompanying certificates of authenticity. Enclosed within another case are vestments worn by Padre Pio. Fr. Denis tells me that this was Padre Pio's study, but I have my doubts. My guess is that it was originally a separate cell, but was converted into the museum, and the wall was opened up to conjoin the two rooms.

Fr. Denis opens the window and tells me to take a look. I stick my head out and am greeted by a wondrous view. I take in the fragrances of the earth and nature, the sounds of the birds (including roosters), and mountainscapes all around. What a wonderful place for a retreat, I think to myself. Fr. Denis shows me several more rooms along the same corridor that are available for guests. I definitely want to stay. As we begin to make our way back down to the courtyard, he offers me a choice of tea or coffee. Before the stairwell, we stop in the choir and admire the craftsmanship of the original flooring. The wood is five centuries old, but appears as if it was recently installed.

As Fr. Denis prepares my espresso (he takes tea), we chat. He tells me he is a collaborator; that is, he is still incardinated in his Province in India and is here on a three-year assignment. There are seven friars from India in this Province, three of which have incardinated. Fr. Denis tells me he spent many years in the missions, mostly in Ethiopia.

"When we traveled, we rode horses. There were no cars or roads. The trails were not in good condition, and I had to jump over puddles or washed-out bridges." I tell him about the massive puddle I just drove through and wish I could have jumped it.

"Why did you come up that road?" he asks perplexed. "You should have taken the road through town." After I blame it on the GPS (not entirely correct), he tells me that he thought that that the road I took was closed. I am sure it is.

He recounts how the years galloping and jumping his horse caused a slipped disc. He had a back operation in Ethiopia that did not go well and, as a result, he has had no feeling in his right leg for thirty-five years.

"It feels like your face when you go to the dentist and get the anesthetic for a tooth. Before, I was athletic and played all the sports – cricket, football, golf, field hockey. I loved sports." I suggest (humbly) that maybe he has been given a penance, like Padre Pio, which he can offer for others. Fr. Denis nods his head.

We finish our caffeinated beverages and step outside. The garden is extensive. As we round a corner, a herd of cats rushes toward Fr. Denis. He struggles to bend down to caress one of them. Then we round another corner and come to a chicken coop. So that's where the crowing has been coming from. We spend some more time gazing out at the mountain views and talking about his country, history, and cultures. Fr. Denis is a real polyglot. He speaks and/or reads twenty languages: ten Indian and ten ancient or European.

We head back to the front of the church and exchange an embrace and *arrivederci*. I point out my mud-coated vehicle. Fr. Denis tells me that in order to get back to the highway, I should go straight toward town and make a left at the first roundabout.

"Don't turn right," he says with a wink.

"I won't."

As I get into my car and wave goodbye to Fr. Denis, I feel an immense sense of gratitude. Thank God for men like Fr. Denis. What a wonderful soul.

I take the civilized road with the switchbacks back down to the highway in the direction of our next stop, Venafro. We will reenter the region of Molise and head in the direction of Isernia covering over 100 kilometers (62 mi). My GPS says the ride should take just over ninety minutes. I check my watch. That will put us there around noon. I hope the friars are still available. Thankfully, most of the route is on a highway – and is straight – and should afford more views as it is in a valley flanked by mountains.

When my GPS says we are four minutes to our destination, I see the ancient village of Venafro in the distance. Perched on the foot of a mountain, it looks charming. A castle dominates the upper part, while ancient city walls still surround the old city. I won't get to see it though, because a few kilometers shy of the old city, we arrive at the Capuchin church and convent complex set immediately off the highway. I make a left directly into the parking lot. Though not in a built-up area (with the exception of the adjacent highway), I assume that, once again, this complex used to be out in the countryside.

I look up at the church. With a rose window in the center of the façade and a prominent bell tower to the left, it has more of a Romanesque or Gothic appearance than Capuchin. It looks like it was once an important abbey or basilica. I know we are in the right place, however, based on a large banner on the bell tower. It says: "The convent that housed Padre Pio of Pietrelcina. Visit the cell and museum." I wonder if the Capuchins acquired this church from one of the monastic orders at some point in the past.

The door to the left of the church, beneath the bell tower, is open. I enter. If the exterior does not have a Capuchin feel, the interior does. It is small, well maintained, and pleasant. The lefthand side beneath the bell tower makes up a minor side aisle, while the main nave is to the right. Above the altar is a very large, wooden *pala d'altare*, or altarpiece. As in Sant'Elia, it comes across as a Spanish retablo. It is adorned with depictions of St. Michael the Archangel,

Mary and the Christ child and angels, and some Capuchin saints. It is embellished with stunning wood inlay. I'm wondering if it was created by the friars. In the past, lay friars (Capuchins not ordained) dedicated themselves to liturgical art, such as woodworking and became masters at the crafts.

The rest of the church is replete with recessed alcoves for niches and statutes. I look around and see Jesus and the Sacred Heart, St. Anthony, Padre Pio, and St. Francis. At the front of the side chapel is a statue of Our Lady. Just like in San Marco la Catola, in the rear is a life-size, cardboard cutout of Venerable Raffaele da Sant'Elia a Pianisi.

I exit the church and ring the bell to the friary. A man with an accent answers and I ask if I can see the cell of Padre Pio. He says he'll buzz me in. The door clicks and pops open slightly. I enter and close it securely behind me. As I wait for the friar, I poke around the courtyard. I examine a pair of old black and white photos of the Venafro convent and church from the early 1900s. I see that there was no bell tower. I also notice that the highway that currently runs alongside the church and convent was a dirt road. There is farmland everywhere else.

I continue walking around the quaint courtyard and come to a sign describing the presence of Padre Pio here. It says:

> In October, 1911, the Provincial Minister, Padre Benedetto da San Marco in Lamis, accompanies Padre Pio to Naples to the well-known Dr. Antonio Cardarelli, who suggests he bring him to Venafro, because the young friar cannot travel long and his days are numbered and... few. During a month and a half spent in Venafro, the fraternity realizes the first supernatural phenomena: ecstasies and diabolical vexations.

After I wait for about ten minutes (and my appetite begins to stir as my nose detects the fragrance of lunch wafting through the courtyard), I wonder if anyone is coming. After another ten minutes (it is now 12:20), I resign myself to the fact that I'm on my own. I see a sign pointing up to the "Padre Pio cell and museum." Since the door is open, I go up, assuming I have been given permission to do so. The staircase leads directly to the cell and museum, which are separated from the cloister by a locked door.

The door to the cell of Padre Pio is also closed and locked. Instead, visitors can peer into the well illuminated room from a broad window that has been retrofitted in one of the walls. Contents are the same as elsewhere: a bed and cross, a porcelain pitcher and water basin, an old chest, a wooden chair and desk, some old books, an oil lantern, and an antiquarian wooden window frame. Adjacent to the cell is a museum, which boasts fewer items than the others. There are: an old, Latin missal and canon, a Eucharistic chalice and paten, and some small relics. In a stand-up encasement are a habit, chasuble, and alb – all worn by Padre Pio. I show myself down and out of the courtyard, and head back into the church.

I sit down and spend a few moments in prayer and reflection. I'm not sure if the highway to my left constitutes noise pollution, but decades ago, it was not here and would not have been a distraction to the friars who had devoted themselves to a strict life of hermitage out in the countryside. Once I am fully confident that no one will be coming out to greet me, I decide to leave. I have to admit to feeling a twinge of disappointment. While I am sensitive to the friars' schedules (midday is marked by prayer, lunch, and rest), I hoped to meet one of them. They have contributed much to my experience in the footsteps of Padre Pio.

Our next stop is Serracapriola. I am hesitant to go for two reasons. First, it is on the opposite side of the Province, at the foothills of the Gargano Mountains on the Adriatic Sea. Venafro, on the other hand, is on the road between Naples and Rome, closer to the Tyrrhenian Sea. My GPS calculates the distance to be 152 kilometers (94 mi) and clocks it at exactly two hours. Given the fact that we will be returning to Pietrelcina this evening – in the center of the Province adding another 120 kilometers (75 mi) – it will make for a very long day. More significantly, I have received mixed reports about Serracapriola. Some say it is open, while others claim it is closed. Regardless, my goal is to visit all ten convents where Padre Pio lived. Even if I can only look at the exterior, I will go.

The route takes us on a state highway across three quarters of the peninsula from the region of Campania through Molise into Abruzzo and then into Puglia. As elsewhere, most of the route is sparsely populated and replete with farmland. I stop for a lunch break at Vasto where I enjoy views of the Adriatic Sea. After some refreshment, I head south along the coast, past Termoli, and then enter the region of northern Puglia. Here we are in the flatlands. This is the famed *Tavoliere delle Puglie* (Apulian table) – a vast and highly cultivated plain. My wife (originally from the region of Puglia) says that these plains are the reason the cuisine from her native region is so rich and varied. Beneath the land are underground springs leading to lush, fertile soil.

I follow the GPS for a short distance and make two left turns off the main road. In front of the convent and church of Serracapriola, the street forms a triangular roundabout. On the right side is a cement wall offering a house some privacy, while a corrugated metal fence does the same for another residence. In the center of the square is an old cross, a statue of Padre Pio, and an inoperative fountain.

The front of the church comes across less as a façade and more an unassuming cream-colored frontage. There is a nondescript window in the upper part and three arches in the bottom creating a slight portico. Forward sloping buttresses have been added to the left and right side of the façade as earthquake reinforcements.

As I park, I notice a gentleman standing outside the church looking around. I make my way toward the church, and him, and hear music. As I get closer, I realize it's coming from a hall next to the church. "What in the world?" I wonder to myself. It sounds like a dance hall.

I approach the gentleman and introduce myself. We shake hands and he tells me his name is Enzo. I ask if the church is open. He says it is not and, in fact, he is waiting for the *responsabile* (the person in charge) to arrive to open up. I ask if the *responsabile* is a friar, to which he responds that the Capuchins are no longer here. After I explain what I'm doing, he says I have come about ten days too late. There were two friars here, but they left on October 5. (Today is October

15.) He says there is still a chance the friars may come back. The Province is having a chapter meeting in February during which they will confirm (or not) the decision to permanently close the friary. In the meantime, the Secular Franciscan fraternity has been given charge of the church where they meet. He is the minister. I ask about the music (inside the hall is a group of dancing kids) and he says they are *eraldini*, (little heralds), a children's group associated with the Secular Franciscans.

As we're speaking, a woman pulls up, parks, and disappears behind a side door. In a few moments, the door to the church opens from within. I acknowledge her and enter. Like most of the other Capuchin churches I have visited in this Province, the interior is in very good condition and lovely. Actually, it is quite beautiful. The main nave is to the right, while to the left is a partial side aisle. The floor is original, likely from the sixteenth century. Above the main altar is a large painting depicting Mary and the Christ child and St. Peter to the side. The walls are painted with scenes from the life of St. Francis on the left and St. Anthony of Padua on the right. As in all the Capuchin churches we have been to, the choir is in the rear above and behind the church. I really love this church.

I approach the altar in search of the tomb of Fra' Matteo Agnone. I have been looking forward to this moment. Instead of a sarcophagus, I discover a plaque on the wall. Behind it, within the wall, there must be an ossuary. It says (in English):

> Here rest the bones of the Servant of God
> Father Matteo da Agnone-Capuchin
> Provincial Minister-Profound Theologian
> Powerful Exorcist, Assertor of the Kingship of Christ
> and of the Assumption of Our Lady
> He had the Gift of Miracles and Prophecies
> He died in the Odor of Sanctity
> In this Convent of Serracapriola
> On October 31, 1616

I go back outside and note a freshly prepared notice on the door of the church declaring that as of October 4, liturgical celebrations here have been suspended, but the church will be kept open from 7:00 AM-12:00 PM, and from 4:00-7:00 PM. Enzo is still standing outside and we speak a little more. After he denies my request to see the convent – "There is no way. We just have keys to the church" – I tell him I think it's sad that the convent is in the process of closing.

"It's not just this one. They want to close six convents." He rattles off the names, four of which I recognize: San Marco la Catola, Venafro, Gesualdo, and Montefusco. I tell him I just went to the first two that morning, Gesualdo yesterday, and will go to Montefusco soon.

He says none of it is official yet, and he hopes that the new Provincial will reverse course. There are "polemics" within the order and community about the closures. He says he cannot understand why they would close this one. Back in the '90s, they spent a lot of *lire* renovating it. The laity is very involved here in Serracapriola, he adds, unlike in some of the other convents. But the fact is that the number of friars is dwindling. The current rule is that there must be at least three friars in each convent. Some people would like to see that number reduced to two in order to keep all the convents open. He says that there are some foreigners, including Indians, and there were also some Africans who were supposed to come, but they didn't. When he was young, all the convents were bustling with friars.

"Not today. Everything's different now."

Before we leave, I notice a plaque on the wall by the door. It says:

> On the centenary of the departure of the young Fra' Pio da Pietrelcina from this convent [1908] in which he was formed in theology in the 90th [year] of his definitive stigmatization, in the fortieth [year] of his blessed transitus, the friars, the people, and the civil authorities, placed [this plaque] as a wish of goodness and development for this land, as a sign of its Christian roots, and as a welcome to Pilgrims. Serracapriola, November 1908-2008

As we make our way back to Pietrelcina, I feel a sense of gratitude. I am pleased I made the trip out here. Though I did not get to see the cell and I missed the friars by just over a week, I am delighted to have seen the church and the tomb of Matteo da Agnone. At the same time, I feel sad. I cannot help but consider the irony in the message posted by the door greeting visitors and pilgrims. Instead of a human (Franciscan) reception, all that remains is a dusty plaque and a happenstance encounter with a wistful layperson. I wonder how much longer this can continue. As is the case in other orders and elsewhere in Italy, Europe, and the West, there is a crisis in vocations. I hate to admit it, but the Province is in serious decline. My journey into the Paschal Mystery has taken me along paths I had not anticipated.

And yet, I must consider that the Paschal Mystery is a journey. We are people of faith: "We know that all things work for good for those who love God, who are called according to his purpose" (Romans 8:28). Yes, God has plans. I think of Scripture: "Then he said to me: Prophesy over these bones, and say to them: Dry bones, hear the word of the LORD! Thus says the Lord GOD to these bones: Listen! I will make breath enter you so you may come to life" (Ezekiel 37:4-5). I make a promise that I will continue praying for holy vocations, confident that God will never disappoint, that he will bring life from death.

Photographs Part I

Figure 1 The Birth Home of St. Padre Pio on Vico Storto Valle 27. It consists of rooms that open to the street (Pietrelcina, Campania)

Figure 2 The church of Sant'Anna where Padre Pio received the sacraments of baptism, first communion, and confirmation (Pietrelcina, Campania)

Figure 3 The Capuchin church and friary where Padre Pio attended his novitiate. He arrived here on January 6, 1903 when he was fifteen years old. (Morcone, Campania)

Figure 4 The interior of the Capuchin church of Sant'Elia a Pianisi. Here Padre Pio began studies (Sant'Elia a Pianisi, Molise)

Figure 5 A black and white picture of Morcone showing what the church and friary looked like a century ago, when Padre Pio arrived.

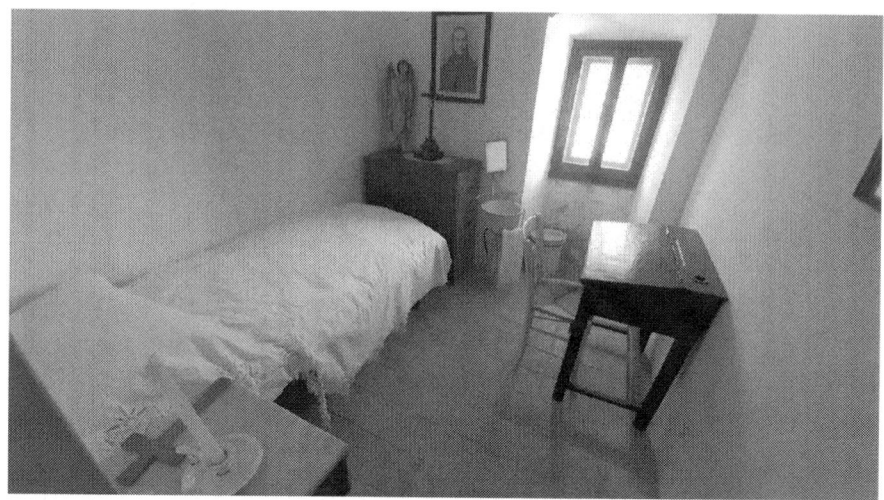

Figure 6 The cell of Padre Pio where he was attacked by a demon in the form of a black dog (Sant'Elia a Pianisi, Molise)

Figure 7 A selfie of Bret Thoman and Fr. Emidio Cappabanca (Gesualdo, Campania)

Figure 8 A photograph of Padre Pio caressing a lamb and Fra' Camillo da Sant'Elia, who died in this friary. Padre Pio was struck by this friar's beard, which led to him wanting to become a Capuchin (Gesualdo, Campania)

Figure 9 A statue in the chapel where Padre Pio was ordained a priest in the cathedral of Benevento (Benevento, Campania)

Figure 10 Fr. Denis Lobo looks after the chickens in the coop just behind the friary (San Marco la Catola, Puglia)

Figure 11 The interior of the Capuchin church of Serracapriola. The church is open to visitors, though the friary is currently closed (Serracapriola, Puglia)

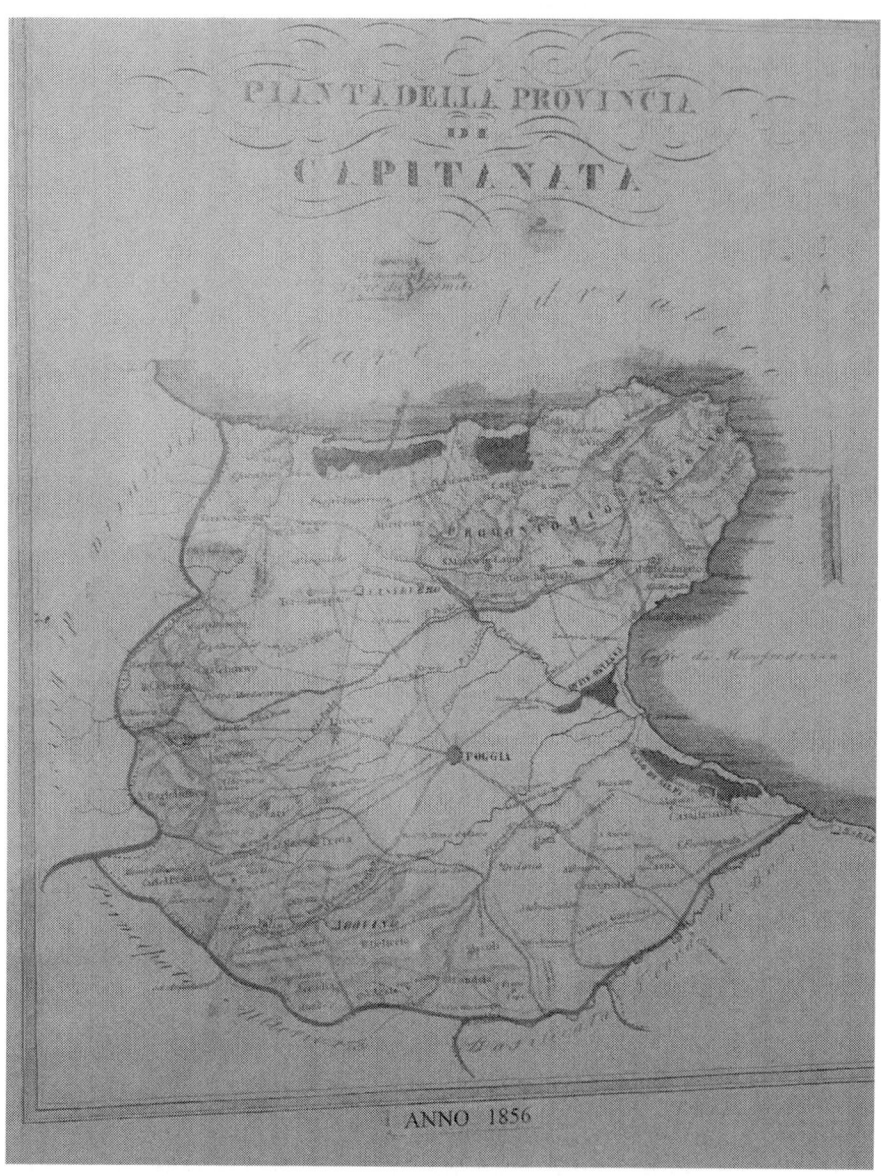

Figure 12 A map from 1856 depicting the friaries within the Capuchin Province of Sant'Angelo (Venafro, Molise)

Part II: From Ordination to Sainthood

10: Priesthood, Victim Soul, and Invisible Stigmata

Four days after Padre Pio's ordination in the cathedral of Benevento, Padre Pio "sung" his first Mass in the church of Our Lady of the Angels at home in Pietrelcina. The day was Sunday, August 14, 1910. Concelebrating at the altar were the parish priest of Pietrelcina and Padre Agostino da San Marco in Lamis. Though he was representing the Minister Provincial, Padre Pio's other spiritual director had an affectionate bond with Padre Pio. It was a day of joy for the entire Province.

It was also a festive celebration for the *Pucinari*, the people of Pietrelcina. They instinctively knew there was something unique about the newly ordained priest among them – Padre Piuccio (Little Pio, as he was known affectionately by the locals). The church was packed. Many had arrived well in advance to ensure they would have a place to sit. When Padre Pio processed into St. Mary of the Angels – vested in splendid, recently embroidered white and gold liturgical vestments – he was preceded by the townspeople. But not everyone remained until the final blessing – especially those standing in the back. The Mass was extraordinarily long; it lasted two hours.

There was something unique about the way Padre Pio celebrated his first Mass. During the Eucharistic prayer, when he asked the Lord to remember the living and the dead, Padre Pio paused and became completely still. Absorbed in prayer, he appeared otherworldly and rapt in prayer. To the amazement of the faithful, after an inordinate amount of time had passed, he resumed the celebration normally, as if his long prayers were only a brief pause. Padre Pio celebrated in such a way because the Holy Mass was at the heart of his new identity. His way of celebrating tapped into the sacrifice that was taking place on the altar, and graces flowed. The celebration of the Eucharistic was at the foundation of what he did, and was, as a priest.

In place of the homily, Padre Agostino spoke about the new priest among them. He knew Padre Pio well through their letters. He said, among other things: "You have poor health; therefore, you will not be a great preacher. However, I wish you to be a great and assiduous confessor." Some believe his words were prophetic. In fact, he never preached. Padre Pio's ministry would consist primarily of three elements: the Mass, reconciliation, and spiritual direction of souls. But the Mass was at the heart of his life and ministry.

After his first Mass, Mamma Peppa distributed the *raffiuoli* she had prepared – traditional Neapolitan sweets distributed to guests on a festive occasion. She also passed out prayer cards with a bible verse and a prayer chosen by the new priest. Padre Pio wanted to communicate in a few words what his priesthood meant to him. The prayer and verse were not randomly selected: he chose them carefully as a summary of how he viewed his ministry:

"*O Rex, dona mihi animam meam pro qua rogo et populum meum pro quo obsecro*"
"If I have found favor with you, O king, if it pleases your majesty, I ask that my life be spared, and I beg that you spare the lives of my people."
(Esther 7:3)

Jesus,
my sigh and my life,
today trembling
I elevate you
in a mystery of love,
with you, may I be for the world
the Way, Truth, and Life

> and for you a holy priest
> [and a] perfect victim.

The verse is from the Book of Esther. Faced with the threat of extermination of her people, Esther pleaded with the king in these words. She begged him to save her people. Like Esther, Padre Pio wished to offer himself as victim. He, too, petitioned his King, so that his ministry would lead to salvation for himself and his people, that is, the people to whom he would minister. To do this, he wished to be a "holy priest and perfect victim." Here one wonders not if Padre Pio understood what he was petitioning, but if he knew what kind of "perfect victim" he would become. In a very short period, he would begin to experience the physical suffering for which he is most known.

The calling of the victim soul is at once mysterious and mystical. Little understood, victim souls freely and voluntarily request to take on sufferings which they offer as a share in the mystical, redemptive power of Christ's Crucifixion and Resurrection. Their pains may manifest themselves visibly or invisibly, and the victims may appear to others pained or joyful. Their sufferings are often accompanied by mystical phenomena such as visions and locutions or other supernatural occurrences. Through these sufferings, victim souls share in Christ's gift of grace which they then extend to others – often for sinners or the sick.

Though every Christian has a "share in the Redemption" and "in his suffering, can also become a sharer in the redemptive suffering of Christ" (see *Salvifici Doloris*, 19, Pope John Paul II), Christ allows certain souls to imitate his suffering more profoundly and closely. Suffering at this level is a particular charismatic calling that must be freely requested and accepted. These are the suffering souls, the victim souls.

In a letter dated November 29, 1910, during which Fra' Pio was tormented by coughing and chest pains, he expressed to the Provincial his wish to become a victim for sinners and souls in purgatory:

> Now, my dear Father, I want to ask your permission for something. For some time past I have felt the need to offer myself to the Lord as a victim for poor sinners and for the souls in Purgatory. This desire has been growing continually in my heart so that it has now become what I would call a strong passion. I have in fact made this offering to the Lord several times, beseeching him to pour out upon me the punishments prepared for sinners and for the souls in a state of purgation, even increasing them a hundredfold for me, as long as he converts and saves sinners and quickly admits to paradise the souls in Purgatory, but I should now like to make this offering to the Lord in obedience to you. (*Letters*, Vol. I, p. 234 - Edizioni Padre Pio da Pietrelcina, 2012)

Padre Benedetto responded to his request affirmatively. In his letter dated December 1, 1910, he sought to prepare his spiritual son for what the role of victim soul would entail:

> Make the offering of which you speak and it will be most acceptable to the Lord. Extend your own arms also on your cross and by offering to the Father the sacrifice of yourself in union with our most loving Savior, suffer, groan and pray for the wicked ones of the earth and for the poor souls in the next life who are so deserving of our compassion in their patient and unspeakable sufferings. (*Letters*, Vol. I, pp. 235-6 - Edizioni Padre Pio da Pietrelcina, 2012)

Those who remained until the end of Padre Pio's first Mass believed its long duration was an exception. They wondered if he had numerous benefactors he wanted to recommend to the Lord, or if he were recalling all those who had led him to this point in his life. Instead, when he celebrated his second and third Masses, it was the same. All his Masses were long. While the first Mass was packed, subsequent liturgies were less so. Most people could not remain for such a long time. They had to go to work in the fields or in their shops. Others had work to do at home. Some even began criticizing him.

But for Padre Pio, the sacrificial nature and dimension of his vocation as a priest was paramount. In those long Masses, he was recommending to the Lord, in a unique way, all the people who were close to him. He not only prayed for his confreres and family members, he began recommending in the sacrifice of the Mass all those who came to him asking for prayers. When he elevated the consecrated Body and Blood of our Lord, he was holding up all the prayers and intentions that had been entrusted to him.

Shortly after his ordination and first Masses, Padre Pio's request to suffer for souls was answered. His suffering increased. First, his scruples returned. The young priest was once again tormented by the idea of offending God and committing sins. He was agitated about whether or not he had confessed all his sins and wondered whether he should make a general confession.

Then, one month after his ordination, Padre Pio experienced something extraordinary. He described it in a letter to Padre Benedetto dated September 8, 1911 (one year after the phenomenon began). This was the first time Padre Pio wrote about these pains. They would come to be known as the invisible stigmata:

> Yesterday evening something happened to me which I can neither explain nor understand. In the center of the palms of my hands a red patch appeared, about the size of a cent and accompanied by acute pain. The pain was much more acute in the left hand and it still persists. I also feel some pain in the soles of my feet. This phenomenon has been repeated several times for almost a year (*Letters*, Vol. I, p. 264 - Edizioni Padre Pio da Pietrelcina, 2012)

Don Salvatore Pannullo – the archpriest, or pastor, of Pietrelcina and Padre Pio's close companion during his sojourn back home – clarified the exact day in which Padre Pio received the stigmata. In a conversation with his niece, Grazia, who learned of the wounds of Padre Pio in 1918, he offered more details. He told her that he had known about them since 1910. He said that Padre Pio received them the first time on Wednesday, September 7, 1910, just under one month after his ordination. In the same conversation, at the repeated requests of his niece who wanted to know more, the priest went on to say that it took place in the plot of land owned by his parents in Piana Romana. More specifically, Padre Pio was seated beneath a large elm tree for prayer and respite from the sun. He often went there for solace and meditation. The following morning when Padre Pio went to St. Mary of the Angels for the celebration of Mass, he told the archpriest everything.

"Zi' 'Tore, do me charity, let us ask Jesus to remove this confusion from me. I want to suffer, to die of suffering, but completely in private."

"My son," Don Pannullo responded, "I will help you to pray and to ask Jesus to remove this confusion from you; however, if it is God's will, you must submit to doing his will in everything and everywhere. And remember, because if this is for the salvation of souls and for the good of the entire world, you must say to Jesus: 'Do with me what you want.'" Following his pastor's counsel, Padre Pio asked Jesus to take away the visible wounds. At once, the outward signs were removed. However, the pains would return from time to time over the following year, especially on certain days of the week.

In a letter dated October 10, 1915, Padre Pio wrote to Padre Agostino describing the reception of the stigmata. (He again speaks of himself as "that soul" in the third person):

> In your second question you ask if he granted this soul the ineffable gift of his holy stigmata. To this the reply must be in the affirmative and the first time Jesus deigned to grant this favor the signs were visible, especially in one hand. The soul was greatly terrified by this phenomenon and therefore asked the Lord to withdraw the visible signs. Since then, the signs are no longer to be seen; however, though the wounds disappeared, the intense pain has not ceased on this account, and it continues especially in certain circumstances and on

certain days. (*Letters*, Vol. I, p. 746 - Edizioni Padre Pio da Pietrelcina, 2012)

In the same letter, Padre Pio revealed to his spiritual director that the Lord allowed him to feel, "many times, his crowning of thorns and his scourging."

In the beginning, God was calling Padre Pio to something that neither he, nor his superiors, initially fully understood. While both Padre Pio – in his request to suffer for souls – and Padre Benedetto – in his affirmative response – were piercing the mystery of the call to redemptive suffering, its link to priesthood would become apparent in time. Padre Pio was being called to an extraordinary mission that was unique among the faithful and priests. He had been gifted with a resemblance to Christ that few priests, if any, had ever experienced. In his desire to become a victim soul and use his sufferings to aid in salvation, Padre Pio was asking to become an *Alter Christus* (another Christ).

Pope Pius XI wrote of the ministry of the priesthood as follows:

> The priest is the minister of Christ, an instrument, that is to say, in the hands of the Divine Redeemer. He continues the work of the redemption in all its world-embracing universality and divine efficacy, that work that wrought so marvelous a transformation in the world. Thus the priest, as is said with good reason, is indeed an *Alter Christus*, "another Christ;" for, in some way, he is himself a continuation of Christ. (Pius XI, *Ad Catholici Sacerdotii*, December 20, 1935)

If all priests are called to be "another Christ," Padre Pio would become a priest like no other. The stigmata he received, albeit temporarily or invisibly, were mystically tied to his priesthood. And both of these were linked to his calling to be a victim soul. The three were linked: priesthood, victim soul, and invisible stigmata. Padre Pio had received the divine gift to offer his physical and mental sufferings – including those of the stigmata – to Christ through the intercession of Our Lady to aid in the salvation of sinners and the sick. He would use his state as a priest and the wounds in a way that had never been done before. He was a priest, Another Christ, like no other. Though they disappeared in this moment, in the future they would return. And they would never disappear until his death.

11: Back to the Order, Foggia

Padre Pio divided his time between town and the countryside of Piana Romana. In Pietrelcina, he lived in the house of his brother, Michele, and performed pastoral work in the parish of Santa Maria degli Angeli. His responsibilities consisted of celebrating Mass and baptizing infants in collaboration with Don Salvatore Pannullo, acting as vicar. In the beginning, Padre Benedetto would not permit him to hear confessions. This prohibition was due to health reasons, in addition to the fact that Padre Pio had not studied moral theology. He would, however, with the permission of his superior, begin offering spiritual direction to laypersons.

In the meantime, Padre Pio's health continued to deteriorate. Not only did he suffer from the invisible stigmata, his illnesses worsened. Eventually, neither the air of his native town nor the numerous medicines he was taking offered him any respite. He was also oppressed by spiritual obsessions and vexations. The more he grew in faith and love for the Lord, the more he was tormented by Satan. He wrote in a letter to Padre Benedetto dated December 20, 1910:

> My dear Father, if it were not for the war which the devil wages against me continually, I should almost be in paradise, but I am in the hands of the devil who is trying to snatch me from the arms of Jesus. Dear God! What a war he is waging against me! (*Letters*, Vol. I, p. 237 - Edizioni Padre Pio da Pietrelcina, 2012)

Over the next few months, the vexations and ill health continued. He wrote to his director begging prayers for the state of his soul and health and lamenting the continual torments by the devil. He also felt temptations regarding impurity and desperation and struggled not to "offend God." During the summer of 1911, there were several days in which he could not get out of bed such that he could not celebrate Mass. This was a tremendous suffering for the newly ordained priest who looked to the Eucharist as the source of his life.

At the same time, Padre Pio also experienced consolations and occasionally felt victorious in his battles with the evil one. In a letter dated August 10, he wrote:

> I am still tormented continually by the snares of the enemy. However, I have noticed in myself for several days now an inexplicable spiritual happiness. I am unaware of the cause of this. I no longer experience the great difficulty I had formerly in resigning myself to God's will. In fact I drive away the tempter's slanderous attacks with such ease that I feel neither annoyed nor wearied. (*Letters*, Vol. I, p. 260 - Edizioni Padre Pio da Pietrelcina, 2012)

As Padre Pio's "temporary" stays in Pietrelcina for native air as a health remedy continued to be extended, his superior (and Padre Pio himself) began to wonder if it would become permanent. Padre Benedetto was becoming increasingly concerned, as he would eventually have to involve the Minister General of the order, as well as the proper Vatican authorities, to continue to allow Padre Pio to remain living outside the cloister. Padre Benedetto became more forceful in his letters. On September 5, he wrote, "If living at home does not cure you, I shall recall you to stay in the shadow of St. Francis. Even if the Lord wants to call you to glory, it is better for you to die in the religious community to which he called you." (*Letters*, Vol. I, pp. 263-4 - Edizioni Padre Pio da Pietrelcina, 2012)

Padre Pio defended himself (in the same letter in which he revealed his reception of the stigmata), on September 8, "The greatest sacrifice I made to the Lord was, in fact, my not being able to live in community. [...] Moreover, I believe that I too have every duty and right not to deprive myself directly of life at twenty-four years of age." (*Letters*, Vol. I, p. 265 - Edizioni Padre Pio da Pietrelcina, 2012) He believed he would die if he left Pietrelcina. At the same time, he declared himself willing to make any sacrifice, as it was a question of obedience. For Padre Pio, the voice of his superiors was the voice of God.

Finally, on September 29, Padre Benedetto insisted that Padre Pio return to the order:

> I repeat that your continued stay in your own home is a source of great sorrow to me. I should not only like to see you in one of our friaries, but here by my side where I could give you the necessary care, for you know my fondness for you as a son. I believe, moreover, that your living outside the cloister no longer serves any purpose, for it is obvious that you are not getting better there. If your illness is God's express will and not a natural fact, then it is better for you to return to the seclusion of holy religion. His native air cannot heal a man who is visited by the Most High and the same man cannot fear to die merely because he is confined to the cloister. Either at home or in the religious community your health will always be as God wills. (*Letters*, Vol. I, pp. 268-9 - Edizioni Padre Pio da Pietrelcina, 2012)

On the feast of St. Francis, October 4, the Provincial became even more forceful. Padre Benedetto wrote to Padre Pio saying that if he did not wish to humbly submit to his judgements, he was doing wrong. He added that if he did not submit to his declarations, he would no longer write him. Padre Pio obeyed. He accepted his orders to return to the order in Morcone, where he had entered the Province as a novice.

From Morcone, Padre Agostino accompanied Padre Pio to Naples to see a specialist, in order "to hear from science if he could remain elsewhere than in his native air without growing worse." The results were positive. The well-known Doctor Antonio Cardarelli believed that Padre Pio could safely return to the convent, because it was not at all necessary for him to "breathe his native air." At this point, Padre Benedetto ordered Padre Pio back to the order, assigning him to the fraternity in Venafro, where he arrived toward the end of October, 1911.

When Padre Pio rejoined his confreres, he was delighted that his other spiritual director, Padre Agostino, was in Venafro teaching a course on preaching. But, once again, he was unable to participate in community life. Shortly after he arrived, Padre Pio's health deteriorated so much that the guardian of the community, Padre Evangelista da San Marco in Lamis, took him back to Naples to see the doctor again. This time his prognosis was not so positive. The two returned to Venafro where Padre Pio could not eat. The little food he was able to ingest was soon regurgitated. He could only receive the Holy Eucharist, which Padre Agostino brought to him at his bedside. He could not even sit up. At the same time, Padre Pio began experiencing vivid diabolical attacks.

Padre Agostino left a diary in which he detailed what he witnessed during Padre Pio's stay in Venafro. He said that when he initially arrived, he was deliriously ill. With some other friars, Padre Pio was lying on the bed with an agitated expression on his face. He told his director to send away a "certain cat" that wanted to fling itself on him. Padre Agostino believed he was close to death, and he went to the choir to pray. When he returned, Padre Pio told him that he did the right thing in going to the choir to pray. "You even thought about my funeral eulogy. There's still time, Padre, there's time."

Padre Agostino detailed the many ways in which the demons appeared to Padre Pio. In addition to taking the form of an ugly, black cat, they appeared as lascivious, dancing women. A third time, they spat in his face without appearing and tormented him with deafening noises. Another time, they appeared as jailers who whipped him. On a fifth occasion, a demon appeared in the form of a crucifix. The next time, the devil appeared as a young man who was a friend of the friars and had recently visited him. On another occasion, the devil took the form of Padre Agostino himself or Pope Pius X. The devil also appeared in the form of Padre Pio's Guardian Angel, St. Francis, Our Lady. Finally, the devil revealed himself in his true form: a horrendous creature with an army of infernal spirits. Padre Pio recognized these apparitions for what they were by ordering the spirits to say, "Long live Jesus!" When they would not, he knew they were demons. After the devil's assaults, Padre Pio was always consoled when Jesus, the Virgin Mary, his Guardian Angel, St. Francis, and other saints appeared to him as their true persons.

Due to the severity of Padre Pio's condition and the fact that he could not even receive water, Padre Benedetto relented and once again agreed to send him back home to Pietrelcina. On December 4, 1911, he signed an order expressing as much. On December 7, Padre Pio left for his native town, accompanied by Padre Agostino. His spiritual director remained with him the next day for the liturgy of the feast of the Immaculate Conception, which Padre Pio concelebrated with Don Salvatore Pannullo. Padre Agostino was amazed to observe him singing with all his strength, as if he had not been sick at all.

Over the following years, Padre Pio's continued to suffer both in body and spirit. At the same time, his charismatic gifts deepened. Beginning in April of the following year, 1912, Padre Agostino began inserting phrases in French in his letters in order to test his spiritual son's spiritual gifts. He noted in subsequent letters (and in his diary), that his Pio understood the language without having ever studied it. On April 20, he wrote to Padre Pio saying, "If possible, will you satisfy my curiosity. Who taught you French?" (*Letters*, Vol. I, p. 310 - Edizioni Padre Pio da Pietrelcina, 2012) Next, on September 7, Padre Agostino wrote an entire letter in Greek. He concluded by asking, "What will your Angel say to this letter? If it pleases God, your Angel could explain it to you. If not, let me know." (*Letters*, Vol. I, p. 341 - Edizioni Padre Pio da Pietrelcina, 2012)

On September 20, Padre Pio responded. He began by recounting the snares the devil – whom, by now, he referred to as *quel cosaccio* (that big, ugly thing) – was playing on him. In conclusion, he wrote (playfully), "And while the mission of our Guardian Angels is a great one, my own Angel's mission is certainly greater, since he has the additional task of teaching me other languages." (*Letters*, Vol. I, p. 343 - Edizioni Padre Pio da Pietrelcina, 2012)

Padre Pio's understanding of Greek was confirmed by the archpriest of Pietrelcina, Don Salvatore Pannullo. At the foot of the September 7 letter from Padre Agostino, written in Greek, he wrote the following testimony:

> Pietrelcina, 25 August 1919. I, the undersigned, testify on oath that when Padre Pio received this letter he explained its contents to me literally. When I asked him how he could read and explain it as he did not know even the Greek alphabet, he replied: "You know! My Guardian Angel explained it all to me." The Archpriest, Salvatore Pannullo (*Letters*, Vol. I, p. 341 - Edizioni Padre Pio da Pietrelcina, 2012)

In addition to the charismatic gift of tongues that was being revealed, around the same time, Padre Pio experienced something else: the piercing of his heart. In a letter on August 26, he wrote to Padre Agostino:

> Listen, now, to what happened to me last Friday [August 23, 1912]. I was in the church making my thanksgiving after Mass, when I suddenly felt my heart wounded by a fiery dart, so sharp and ardent that I thought I should die. [...] It seemed to me as if an invisible power were plunging my whole being into fire. [...] I have experienced a great many of these transports of love, and for some time have remained, as it were, outside this world. On the other occasions, however, this fire was less intense, whereas this time another moment, another second, and my soul would have been separated from my body and would have gone to Jesus." (*Letters*, Vol. I, p. 338 - Edizioni Padre Pio da Pietrelcina, 2012)

In practical matters, Padre Pio's situation was becoming more dire. The Minister General was now directly involved. Padre Pacifico da Seggiano had been made fully aware of the situation – in which a fully professed friar and priest had been living outside the convent for an extended period of time. He had to intervene. Initially, he suggested the most extreme option, that of secularization. This meant that Padre Pio would be deprived of the habit and forced out of the order. If such a decision had been confirmed, to remain a priest, Padre Pio would have been forced to find another ordinary or ecclesiastical superior to take him. He would have had to enter another order or become a diocesan priest among the secular clergy.

When Padre Pio discovered that the Minister General had communicated to Padre Benedetto that he would ask for a brief of secularization, he was terrified. But St. Francis appeared to him and consoled him in a vision. Padre Pio lamented to St. Francis that he was being thrown out of his order: "My father, for charity's sake, let me die instead!" St. Francis revealed to him that he would retain the habit. Indeed, such was the case. The Minister General did not carry through with his threat.

Over the next three years – filled with misunderstandings and trials on both the part of the Provincial and Padre Pio – a compromise was reached. Both Padre Agostino and Padre Benedetto met and spoke with the General who agreed to seek from the Vatican Congregation for Religious, a brief referred to as, *ad tempus, habitu retentor*. This meant that Padre Pio could continue to temporarily reside outside the order (*ad tempus*), while continuing to wear the Capuchin habit (*habitu retentor*). On December 14, 1914, Padre Benedetto explained to his spiritual son the decision, and added that Pio should contact the archbishop of Benevento to ensure he could continue celebrating Mass and accept him, provisionally, as belonging to the clergy of Pietrelcina.

Though Padre Pio was not excommunicated from the order, he felt humiliated. In a letter to Padre Agostino on December 19, 1914, he wrote:

> It is a great humiliation for me, dear Father, to see myself almost cut off from the Seraphic Order. The pain is so acute that although I had prepared myself for this it overwhelmed me the moment I received the Provincial's letter telling me

what had been decided. The abundant tears I shed were also very injurious to my health, so that I was obliged to go to bed where I still am as I write. (*Letters*, Vol. I, p. 581 - Edizioni Padre Pio da Pietrelcina, 2012)

In his response, Padre Agostino reassured him that it was a temptation to consider himself "cut off from the Order, [...] The General recognized the divine will and he grants you the Brief of Exclaustration while you are still to wear the seraphic habit, so you continue to belong to us and even more so to our Seraphic Father." (*Letters*, Vol. I, p. 583 - Edizioni Padre Pio da Pietrelcina, 2012)

Padre Pio's stay at home would last another fourteen months. The only exception was when he was called to military service. By now Italy had entered World War I. On May 23, 1915, Italy declared war on Austria-Hungary and entered the Great War on the side of the Allies – Britain, France and Russia. Padre Pio was twenty-eight years old. While the Lateran Treaty of 1929 eventually exempted Italian priests and fully vowed religious from military service (save in case of general mobilization), World War I took place during the Suppression of the Italian Church. Priests or religious were not exempt from military service. Padre Pio's Province, in fact, would soon be drained as thirty friars – all of military age – were conscripted.

Thus, on November 6, 1915, Padre Pio presented himself for duty at the Commissariat in Benevento. After submitting to a rigorous medical exam by a "ferocious medical captain," Pio was diagnosed with tuberculosis and promptly sent to the observation ward in a military hospital in Caserta. After another evaluation, he was sent to Naples, arriving on December 6. After waiting eleven days for yet another evaluation (during which time he had to pay for his own room and board!), Padre Pio was examined and received the news that he was not fit for service due to his ill health. He had a "lung infiltration," and was given leave for one year. He returned home.

Though Padre Pio was relieved to be back in Pietrelcina, divine plans were underway. In a letter (written in French) on June 22, 1913,

Padre Agostino mentioned two women with whom he was in contact. He asked him to pray for these two souls who had recommended themselves to his prayers. One of these women would have an important impact on Padre Pio's life in many ways. Eventually, she would mark the beginning of his ministries to his devoted spiritual daughters. In the short term, she would be instrumental in his relocation back into the order. Her name was Raffaella Cerase.

Through his work with her, Padre Pio found himself called to a new form of ministry: spiritual direction via epistolary correspondence – an "apostolate of the pen." On March 24, 1914, Raffaella wrote him her first letter. She began by saying, "Jesus has sent me to you and after having asked permission and obtained leave – spontaneously, fully and without limits – from my confessor and yours, I have decided to write you." (*Letters*, Vol. II, p. 63 - Edizioni Padre Pio da Pietrelcina, 2019)

Raffaelina, as she was usually known – or Lellina affectionately – was a tertiary in the Third Order of St. Francis and a member of the women's section of Catholic Action. Born in the city of Foggia on November 1, 1868, she was of noble lineage. She lived near the Capuchin Church of Sant'Anna with her older sister, Giovina, who was like a second mother to her.

Following the suggestion of Padre Agostino, Pio agreed to guide her spiritually via correspondence. The ninety-eight letters exchanged between Padre Pio and Raffaelina Cerase make up the entirety of the second volume of the *Letters of Padre Pio*. They are profound in spirituality and present an intimate portrait of how Padre Pio guided souls. In a long letter dated October 23, 1914, the day before the feast of St. Raphael and namesake of Raffaelina, Padre Pio wrote a letter so dense in spiritual wisdom and counsel that it is a veritable treatise in spiritual direction.

In autumn of 1915, Raffaelina was diagnosed with cancer, and in October, she had an operation. Subsequently, she became very ill. Sensing death was approaching and having been under Padre Pio's direction exclusively via letters for almost two years, she had a fervent desire to see her spiritual director in person and confess to him. She beseeched Padre Agostino for the occasion to be able to meet him.

In the meantime, Padre Benedetto was still searching for a way to bring Padre Pio back into the order, and perhaps the events with Raffaelina could be an opportunity to do so. On Thursday, February 17, 1916, Padre Pio met Padre Agostino at the train station in Benevento to accompany him to Foggia. He did not dare meet him in Pietrelcina, as he feared the reaction of the *Pucinari* and how they might resist having their saint "stolen" from them. Once in Foggia, Padre Agostino accompanied Pio to the Capuchin convent at the church of Sant'Anna (St. Ann's). Convinced that his stay in Foggia was to last only several days, Padre Pio was about to learn otherwise. No sooner did he set foot within the convent than the Provincial Minister met him. He was there on an official visit to the community, which, however, was probably timed to coincide with Pio's arrival. Padre Benedetto da San Marco da Lamis – in the role of superior – stated in clear terms: "You shall no longer leave here. You will stay in the convent forever, dead or alive."

Padre Pio obediently handed over the little money he had with him for his return ticket, withdrew to his assigned cell, and wrote to the archpriest of Pietrelcina informing him of his new situation. Likewise, he wrote to his mother asking her to send his personal effects to his new home. He would never again return to Pietrelcina.

12: From the Plains to the Mountains

Once settled in his cell in Foggia, Padre Agostino accompanied Pio to the house of Raffaelina Cerase. Close to the convent, Padre Pio visited his spiritual daughter daily and sat at her bedside. He would spend hours with her and sometimes celebrate Mass in her private chapel, dedicated to the Sacred Heart of Jesus. He continued this for the next five weeks.

On March 25, 1916, Padre Pio took out his pen and paper and wrote to Padre Agostino – the person responsible for his relationship with Raffaelina: "This morning at four o'clock we gained another intercessor at the throne of the Most High. Raffaelina has finished the course, she has celebrated the nuptials with her divine Spouse. She fell asleep in the Lord with a smile of contempt for this world. Lucky soul!" (*Letters*, Vol. I, p. 860 - Edizioni Padre Pio da Pietrelcina, 2012)

Though the motive for his assignment in Foggia was now fulfilled, Padre Pio remained in the fraternity in the northern Apulian city for seven months. Padre Benedetto remained firm: Pio would stay in the convent in Foggia. Perhaps some of it was due to Raffaelina. Before her death, the holy woman had insisted to Padre Agostino that Padre Pio should remain in the friary: "Make him return and let him hear confessions as he will do much good!" she said.

In Foggia, Padre Pio came into contact with other laypersons hungering for spiritual direction, and he began counseling and guiding them. He soon found himself in growing demand, and crowds of people began flocking to him. In a letter to Padre Agostino on August 23, 1916, Pio wrote:

> Moreover, I must let you know that I am not left a free moment: crowds of people thirsting for Jesus are pressing upon me, so that I am at my wit's end. In face of such an abundant harvest, on the one hand, I feel glad in the Lord because I see the ranks of chosen souls swelling and love for Jesus growing; on the other hand, I am dismayed by such a burden. (*Letters*, Vol. I, p. 896 - Edizioni Padre Pio da Pietrelcina, 2012)

During his stay in Foggia, Padre Pio's health ailments continued. So did his struggle with demons. The guardian of the community, Padre Nazareno d'Arpaise, kept a notebook replete with numerous anecdotes about Padre Pio's stay in the community. Toward the beginning of his stay, the friars were not accustomed to spiritual interventions of this sort. In fact, the extraordinary phenomena surrounding Padre Pio had been kept secret by his spiritual directors and the few friars who were aware of them. In Foggia, they could no longer be guarded. While the demons had previously manifested themselves in visions, they now became physical … and noisy.

During suppertime, which Padre Pio rarely attended and instead retired to his cell, the friars began to hear noises coming from the ceiling, as his cell was immediately above the refectory. When they went to check on him, he would appear cheerful in their presence, but soaked with perspiration. While the phenomena initially frightened them, they soon became accustomed to the spiritual battles.

Visitors from outside the community, however, were not accustomed to the phenomena surrounding the young friar's life. Padre Nazareno described the arrival of a bishop who came to Foggia with his assistant and a Capuchin friar. Though he had been warned of the events taking place in Padre Pio's cell, the bishop scoffed. He believed that such events no longer took place in modern times. The guardian wrote:

> One evening, Monsignor D'Agostino, Bishop of Ariano Irpino, dropped into the friary [with plans to stay the night]. I thought it best to inform him of what was happening to which he said: "Father Guardian, the medieval age is over but you still believe in that nonsense." Very well, I said in my heart, that man is like Thomas the Apostle who didn't believe without seeing, but he will believe it! The supper bell rang and we went to the refectory. We were dispensed from the usual silence in honor of our guest, and while everyone talked, I heard a banging, which I always noticed before the noise, on the ceiling of the refectory. I asked for silence and then the noise followed. The bishop's domestic help who was eating in the guest quarters, terrified, ran with his hair standing on end into the refectory. The bishop was so frightened that he did not want to sleep alone that night, and the following day he left the friary and never returned.

In addition to the spiritual attacks Padre Pio was enduring, he was also suffering from the intense summer heat. Foggia is located at a low altitude on the plains inland from the sea and is excruciatingly hot and humid during the summers. Padre Pio lamented that he could find no "refreshment." As it happened, Padre Paolino da Casacalenda, the guardian of the friary in San Giovanni Rotondo up in the Gargano Mountains, was in Foggia preaching a novena in honor of St. Ann. Seeing Padre Pio suffering so, he invited him to spend a few days with him up in the convent for respite from the heat. The fraternity consisted of several professed friars and a community of students in formation. That invitation was providential in many ways.

Having obtained permission from Padre Nazzareno, the two Capuchins left. Padre Pio arrived in San Giovanni Rotondo the first time on the evening of July 28, 1916. As the two ascended the

Gargano Mountains, he immediately found respite from the heavy air down in Foggia and sensed the pristine environment would be good for his lungs. Its high elevation at 565 meters sea level (1,850 feet) and mountain climate rendered the air decisively cooler and more crisp.

Overlooking the Capuchin complex a few kilometers to the northeast was the towering Mount Calvo. At 1054 meters sea level (3500 ft), it is the highest peak in the Gargano Mountain range. About twenty-two kilometers (13 mi) to the southeast, out of view, sit the city and Gulf of Manfredonia. The same distance to the east is the famed sanctuary of St. Michael the Archangel, an important pilgrimage site since the Middle Ages and especially during the period of the crusaders. Padre Pio looked around. He knew that San Giovanni Rotondo would benefit more than his lungs. He was instinctively drawn to the place and knew that something important would take place here.

In the Gargano peninsula – just as in all the small villages throughout the territory – the people were poor. The homes had no electricity, no potable water, and no sewage. There were no paved roads or means of modern communication, such as the telephone or even the telegraph. The Capuchin community was not much better off. The church and friary were in poor shape. But for Padre Pio, it was perfect.

The friary and church were set far from the village, connected by little more than a mule track. Few people ventured out to the complex surrounded by rocky, barren land. The soil was too stony for farming, and the only trees that grew well there were almond and fig trees. Other than the occasional pastor and flocks of sheep, the Capuchin friars of San Giovanni Rotondo were blessed with solitude and seclusion that marked their charism.

The barren setting was described in a letter by a friar named Padre Isaia da Sorno who visited the convent and church of San Giovanni Rotondo in 1915:

> Far from the village, people rarely came to the church; profound silence surrounds me and only now and then do I

hear the clang of bells which hang on the necks of some goats or sheep, which the shepherds bring to the mountain behind the friary to graze.

The presence of the Capuchin Friars Minor in San Giovanni Rotondo dated back to 1540 when the land was donated to the Province by a nobleman named Orazio Antonio Landi. Initially, their convent consisted of little more than a country house and a well, typical of rural farms in the Apulian countryside. Soon, a proper church and convent were built and consecrated and dedicated to Santa Maria delle Grazie (Our Lady of Grace). Due to its remote location, the site initially served as the novitiate for the Province.

The structures had not been fundamentally altered in many centuries when Padre Pio arrived. The convent was buttressed up against the church of Santa Maria delle Grazie, while an old stone wall enclosed the perimeter of the complex. There was a small cross, still present today in the parvis of the ancient church, along with an ancient icon of Our Lady of Grace, which still adorns the main altar in the ancient church. Though the friary and church date to the sixteenth century, it had only been recently reopened when Padre Pio arrived. Along with so many other churches and convents during the Suppression of the Catholic Church, the friary of San Giovanni Rotondo was closed.

The fresh mountain air had an immediate effect on Padre Pio. Those few days on the slopes of the Gargano brought great relief to his lungs. His first sojourn in San Giovanni Rotondo only lasted one week, however. He did not want to stay longer, as he fretted that he had not had the express consent of the Provincial.

Back in Foggia, on August 13, Padre Pio wrote a long letter to Padre Benedetto, in which he communicated his suffering caused by the heat, and mentioned other ailments including vision problems, dizziness, and fevers. He then asked his superior for a "favor," which he believed "Jesus had compelled him to do." He asked his superior to allow him to spend some time in San Giovanni Rotondo.

In his response on August 17, Padre Benedetto said that he had given his permission to the guardian for him to go, at least provisionally. He wrote that he hoped he would "soon return and be able to go to the mountains." However, the guardian, Padre Nazareno d'Arpaise, had been called to military service, and a minimum of two friars needed to staff the community in Foggia. When Padre Isaia da Sarno arrived to take his place, Padre Pio could leave for San Giovanni Rotondo. The date was September 4, 1916.

Pio settled in gracefully. Padre Paolino, the guardian, wrote that he initially occupied himself by reading ascetic books and Sacred Scripture and directing souls. In addition to continued spiritual direction of laypersons in Foggia and Pietrelcina via correspondence, he began offering spiritual direction to his confreres who went to him for confession. When his health was poor, he would offer his suffering as a victim for the benefit of others.

Padre Pio remained in the friary in San Giovanni Rotondo with a few exceptions. On May 16, 1917, he made a short trip to Rome to accompany his younger sister to the convent – the only time he ever visited the Eternal City (physically). At the age of twenty-two, Graziella entered the Brigidine monastery, taking the name, Sister Pia dell'Addolorata. Padre Benedetto accompanied them, and the two friars used the occasion to visit the basilicas of the city.

On July 1, Padre Pio accompanied the students on foot for a pilgrimage to the nearby sanctuary of Monte Sant'Angelo – the famed apparition site of St. Michael the Archangel, which gave its name to the Capuchin Province. Though it was a grueling day, Padre Pio was delighted as he always had a deep devotion to St. Michael. Later, he would often send the faithful to the grotto for penance after hearing their confessions.

Padre Pio's stay in the community of San Giovanni Rotondo was interrupted more substantially when he was called back to military service on three more occasions. Before leaving, he renewed his request for prayers to all those who could recommend him to "be freed, soon this time, from the saga of the military." The third and final time Padre Pio was called back to the military was the worst form of penance. He described his experience in the military as a "madhouse," in which there were constant swearing, obscenities and blasphemies. He was assigned humiliating and tiring tasks as attendant, sweeper, and porter, and he referred to himself as a "wrong soldier." Worst of all, he was forced to remove his Capuchin habit and don the clumsy military uniform. Finally, his health was so poor that the military doctors concluded that Padre Pio had no more than fifteen days to live. They discharged him to "allow him to die in peace at home." On March 16, 1918, he was given his final leave, having been diagnosed with double bronchus alveolitis. Padre Pio could once again return to his isolated mountain convent in San Giovanni Rotondo. This time he would never leave.

While the people of San Giovanni Rotondo who met the friar from Pietrelcina recognized there was something particular about him, no one had any idea what was about to happen. The events that transpired over the next six months were marked by a series of mystical and extraordinary phenomena of such magnitude that San Giovanni Rotondo would soon be transformed from a sleepy, backwater village into one of the foremost pilgrimage destinations in all Christendom. Padre Pio would soon become a household name – in San Giovanni Rotondo, throughout Italy, and beyond.

13: The Permanent Stigmata

Two months after Padre Pio's permanent return to San Giovanni Rotondo, he felt an ardent desire to pray for a particular cause: the end to the war. On May 30, 1918, during the Mass of the Feast of Corpus Domini, Padre Pio offered himself to the Lord for the cessation of all hostilities. Then, he received what is referred to as the "substantial touch." He described it in a letter on July 27, 1918 to Padre Benedetto:

> Here is what happened to me on that day. During my Mass in the morning [on Corpus Domini: May 30, 1918], I was touched by a living breath. I cannot convey the slightest idea of what happened within me in that fleeting moment. I felt completely shaken, filled with extreme terror and I almost passed away. This was followed by a state of total calm such as I had never before experienced. This terror, agitation and calm in quick succession were not caused by the sight of anything but by something which I felt touching me in the deepest recesses of my soul. I am unable to say any more about this occurrence. May God be pleased to make you understand what really happened to me. While this was taking place I had time to offer myself entirely to the Lord for the same intention which the Holy Father [Pope Benedict XV] had when he recommended to the whole Church to offer prayers and sacrifices. I had hardly finished doing so when I felt myself falling into this most harsh prison and heard the

loud clang of the prison door as it closed behind me. Cruel shackles seemed to close on me and bind me tightly and I felt I was about to die. Since that moment I have felt myself in hell without even an instant's respite. (*Letters*, Vol. I, p. 1173 - Edizioni Padre Pio da Pietrelcina, 2012)

Two months later, a second extraordinary event took place. On August 5, on the Vigil of the Feast of the Transfiguration, he received what is known as the transverberation; that is, the piercing of the heart. In a letter dated August 21, 1918 to Padre Benedetto, he wrote:

For this reason I am led to manifest to you what happened to me on the evening of the 5th of this month and all day on the 6th. I am quite unable to convey to you what occurred during this period of utter torment. While I was hearing the boys' confessions on the evening of the 5th, I was suddenly terrorized by the sight of a celestial person who presented himself to my mind's eye. He had in his hand a sort of weapon like a very long sharp-pointed steel blade which seemed to emit fire. At the very instant that I saw all this, I saw that person hurl the weapon into my soul with all his might. I cried out with difficulty and felt I was dying. I asked the boy to leave because I felt ill and no longer had the strength to continue. This agony lasted uninterruptedly until the morning of the 7th. I cannot tell you how much I suffered during this period of anguish. Even my entrails were torn and ruptured by the weapon, and nothing was spared. From that day on I have been mortally wounded. I feel in the depths of my soul a wound that is always open and which causes me continual agony. (*Letters*, Vol. I, p. 1186 - Edizioni Padre Pio da Pietrelcina, 2012)

By now, Padre Benedetto recognized the spiritual nature of Padre Pio's illnesses and sufferings. He was convinced that these particular phenomena were supernatural, and that God was using him and his sufferings in a particular way. In his response on August 27, he wrote that all that was happening to Padre Pio was due to the "effect of love" and his "vocation to co-redemption." He said that Jesus is "associated with your suffering and [he] associates you with his own." He added that Padre Pio's suffering was not a "purgation but a painful union." He concluded the letter, saying, "Kiss the hand that has pierced you through and cherish most tenderly this wound which is the pledge of love."

Padre Benedetto was the first to use this word, transverberation, (Ita: *trasverberato*; translated "pierced you through" in English) in relation to what happened to Padre Pio while hearing the confession of the student. St. John of the Cross used the word in his spiritual treatise, *The Living Flame of Love*, written in 1585:

> It will happen that while the soul is inflamed with the love of God it will feel that a seraph is assailing it by means of an arrow or dart which is all afire with love. And the seraph pierces and cauterizes this soul which, like a red-hot coal, or better a flame, is already enkindled. And then in this cauterization, when the soul is transverberated with that dart, the flame gushes forth, vehemently and with a sudden ascent, like the fire in a furnace or an oven when someone uses a poker or bellows to stir and excite it.

It could be said that the transverberation received by St. Padre Pio was a prelude to the final, most extraordinary event. What was about to take place had already happened, even if provisionally, eight years earlier, shortly after Pio's ordination to the priesthood. While the wounds were initially temporary and invisible in 1910, this time, they would remain permanent. Padre Pio would bear the wounds of Christ on his body for fifty years. They would heal only shortly before he died.

The stigmatization took place on Friday, September 20, at 9:00 AM. The other two professed friars were outside the convent, while the students were at recreation in the courtyard. Padre Pio was praying before the wooden crucifix in the choir above the ancient church giving thanks after the morning Mass. He was alone. He described it in a letter to Father Benedetto written a month later, on October 22:

> On the morning of the 20th of last month, in the choir, after I had celebrated Mass, I yielded to a drowsiness similar to a sweet sleep. All the internal and external senses and even the very faculties of my soul were immersed in indescribable stillness. Absolute silence surrounded and invaded me. I was suddenly filled with great peace and abandonment which effaced everything else and caused a lull in the turmoil. All this happened in a flash. While this was taking place I saw before me a mysterious person similar to the one I had seen on the evening of 5 August. The only difference was that his hands and feet and side were dripping blood. This sight terrified me and what I felt at that moment is indescribable. I thought I should die and really should have died if the Lord had not intervened and strengthened my heart which was about to burst out of my chest. The vision disappeared and I became aware that my hands, feet and side were dripping blood. (*Letters*, Vol. I, pp. 1217-18 - Edizioni Padre Pio da Pietrelcina, 2012)

Compared to the wounds he received in Piana Romana shortly after ordination, these wounds were more pronounced. They bled profusely to the point that he feared he would bleed to death. Once again, they were a deep source of embarrassment and humiliation, and he begged God to take away the external signs. However, unlike in Pietrelcina, this time the Almighty did not grant his request. They would not disappear until his death, a half century later to the day.

> Imagine the agony I experienced and continue to experience almost every day. The heart wound bleeds continually, especially from Thursday evening until Saturday. Dear Father, I am dying of pain because of the wounds and the resulting embarrassment I feel deep in my soul. I am afraid I shall bleed to death if the Lord does not hear my heartfelt

supplication to relive me of this condition. Will Jesus, who is so good, grant me this grace? Will he at least free me from the embarrassment caused by these outward signs? I will raise my voice and will not stop imploring him until in his mercy he takes away, not the wound or the pain, which is impossible since I wish to be inebriated with pain, but these outward signs which cause me such embarrassment and unbearable humiliation. (Ibid.)

Padre Pio tried to keep his wounds secret, but was unsuccessful. The next day, he was visited by one of his spiritual daughters, Nina Campanile from San Giovanni Rotondo. Though Padre Pio tried to hide the wounds, she noticed them and understood what they were. She went home and told her mother and sister that Padre Pio had the stigmata "like St. Francis." She also told the guardian, Padre Paolino.

Padre Paolino went directly to cell number five to see for himself. He, too, witnessed the sores on the back and palm of Padre Pio's right hand and the one on the back of the left. He could not see the wound on his left palm as it was resting on the table. He promptly wrote a letter to the Provincial, Padre Benedetto, informing him of what happened. His superior responded by telling him to keep the greatest silence. At the same time, Padre Benedetto wrote to Padre Pio ordering him to tell him everything clearly and in holy obedience. On October 22, 1918, Padre Pio took his pen and paper and wrote to his spiritual director the letter referenced above.

What happened to Padre Pio of Pietrelcina in San Giovanni Rotondo on September 20, 1918 is uniquely and spiritually linked to what happened to his baptismal namesake and founder of the Franciscan Order some seven centuries earlier. On September 17, three days before Padre Pio received his wounds, the Franciscan Order celebrates the Feast of the Stigmata of St. Francis. Three days before that, on September 14, the Catholic Church celebrates the Feast of the Exaltation of the Cross. It is too coincidental to consider that the feasts of the cross and St. Francis's reception of it on his body were not somehow connected to what happened to Padre Pio on that September 20 morning.

St. Francis' reception of the stigmata has been interpreted as a seal imprinted on his body to signify God's approval of his life and mission. He received it two years before he died. By then, he had perfected charity by practicing virtues, serving others, and loving God.

In a letter to the order written in 1226, shortly after St. Francis' death, Br. Elias described the reception of the stigmata. He wrote: "Such a sign that has never been heard of from the dawn of time except in the Son of God, who is Christ the Lord." No one had ever heard of such a thing. The reception of the stigmata – the wounds of Christ – on the body of one of the faithful was a novelty in the history of Christianity. Though it cannot be said that no one had ever received Christ's wounds previously – in his letter to the Galatians, St. Paul wrote (using the same Greek word), "I bear on my body the [stigmata] of Jesus" (6:17) – what happened to St. Francis in 1224 is the first time the reception of the stigmata were ever recorded or identified as such.

The word, stigmata, is Greek in origin and means simply, "marks or spots." If St. Francis was the first to receive the stigmata, he was not the last. In the centuries that followed the High Middle Ages, numerous mystics have received the wounds of Christ or some form thereof. St. Catherine of Siena, for example, received the five marks in the fourteenth century. Other saints and mystics have received Christ's wounds partially. St. Rita of Cascia received a wound to her forehead, recalling one of the thorns of the crown. Others, like St. Faustina Kowalska, received the invisible stigmata in which they felt the wounds on their members, but without a physical or external sign.

If Padre Pio was not the only person to have received the wounds, he was the first priest to have received them. In fact, he may be the only stigmatic priest, as no other priest is known to have borne the wounds of Christ. St. Francis received diaconal orders, not sacerdotal. No other stigmatic has had, thus, the faculties to consecrate the Eucharist or forgive sins. Only Padre Pio has.

Regarding his priestly ordination, Padre Pio was no different from any other priest from the time of Christ. When his soul was indelibly marked with holy orders, he received the same sacerdotal faculties to consecrate the Eucharist, forgive sins, anoint the sick, and bless in the name of the Trinity. Like all priests, his ordination conferred on him the state of acting *in Persona Christi* (in the Person of Christ) when administering the sacraments. That is, when a priest consecrates the Eucharist, forgives sins, and blesses the faithful, he is not acting as a vicar of Christ, but in the Person of Christ. The priest becomes an *Alter Christus*, another Christ.

And yet, Pio's body was also signed with the marks of Christ's Passion, the stigmata. While Padre Pio famously said (more than once) that he (and his stigmata) were a mystery to himself, there is a particular message in the way God intervened in Padre Pio so profoundly. While St. Francis received the marks at the end of his life, interpreted as a sign of God's confirmation on it – one may ask whether God wished to highlight the sacrificial dimension of the priesthood, since he received the wounds at the same time he was ordained. The stigmata of Padre Pio, hence, has been read as God's way of showing the Church – and the world – the true identity of the priest.

Or, it may be that God willed the miracles in the life of Padre Pio for other reasons. Indeed, once word got out that a priest in the Gargano Mountains had received the stigmata, people were immediately drawn to him. While many came initially out of curiosity, once they drew near, they were struck. San Giovanni Rotondo soon became the scene of innumerable conversions, healings, and miracles.

14: Forever in San Giovanni Rotondo

Word of the presence of a young Capuchin friar stamped with the wounds of Christ spread throughout San Giovanni Rotondo, the Gargano and surrounding area, and beyond. Padre Pio attempted to hide the marks with the sleeves of his habit or liturgical vestments, but to no avail. His humility only served to increase people's belief in the rumor that was on everyone's lips: there was a saint in their midst.

Crowds began flocking to the convent. Everyone wanted to see Padre Pio and his wounds. While many were simple peasants, others were people of culture. Some came out of curiosity, as if to a circus, while others arrived hoping for special graces and miracles. They beseeched him to intercede and pray for a sick family member, a wayward husband or grown son, or a resolution to crushing poverty.

On February 28, 1919, the Provincial Minister came to San Giovanni Rotondo to see for himself. After Padre Benedetto observed the stigmata personally, he decided to call a doctor to examine them. Dr. Luigi Romanelli came from Barletta and offered a favorable conclusion: "The etiology of Padre Pio's injuries being of natural origin must be excluded. The producing agent, instead, must be sought in the supernatural without fear of error."

Respected Italian newspapers picked up the scoop and began running articles about a friar "crucified like Jesus" and the "Gargano saint," with headlines such as, "the Man Who Works Miracles." It wasn't long before the Minister General of the order heard. So did the Holy See.

More doctors were sent to investigate. One attempted to treat the wounds, to no avail. Some believed the stigmata were caused unconsciously through psychological conditions referred to as "hysteria" or "auto-suggestion." Others believed that Padre Pio had created the wounds himself by applying chemical compounds such as iodine or carbolic acid.

Dr. Amico Bignami, from the esteemed Sapienza University in Rome, suggested an experiment. He recommended the guardian have the wounds bandaged and sealed in the presence of witnesses. Each day, for eight days, the seals were to be checked for signs of tampering. This was to ensure the wounds had not been touched in any way, much less treated. The experiment was conducted as instructed. On the eighth day, when the friars removed the bandages, they discovered the wounds had not changed at all. In fact, they remained the same as when the bandages were applied. This is against the course of nature: an open wound will either heal or get worse; it will not remain the same.

As word spread, more people came. Skeptics wanted to see for themselves, while believers wanted to confess to the stigmatized saint. New levels of organization had to be implemented, and the friars rearranged the confessionals. Two were set up in the sacristy for the men, and one in the nave for the women. This way, other friars or priests passing through could hear confessions. But it didn't work. The people wanted to confess to Padre Pio. People began camping out in front of the convent and even sleeping inside the church. They waited ten to fifteen days to confess to the stigmatized Capuchin. Law enforcement now got involved with crowd control measures, and the friars began scheduling calendar appointments for confession.

Now newspapers from across the Alps caught wind of the story, and articles about the Italian priest with the marks of Christ were published in English, French, Flemish, and Spanish. Telegrams and letters began to arrive by the truckload, first from all over Italy then from all over the world. They were postmarked in France, Spain,

England, and even the United States. Against his will, Padre Pio had been thrust into international fame.

He tried not to be overwhelmed by the events and remain humble, and he began covering his wounds with fingerless gloves and socks. He spent most of his time in the confessional, hearing confessions for up to sixteen hours a day. He strived to receive everyone who came to him, even when he felt weak or unwell. He wrote to his spiritual director on October 23, 1921: "I have worked and I intend to work; I have prayed and I intend to pray; I have kept watch and I intend to keep watch; I have wept and I intend always to weep for my brothers in exile." (*Letters*, Vol. I, p. 1389 - Edizioni Padre Pio da Pietrelcina, 2012) However, there were too many people. It was not possible to receive everyone.

While most people came to San Giovanni Rotondo out of sincerity, there were those who came for less noble reasons. Some were curious. Padre Pio had no time to be patient with these people, and his brusqueness began to surface. Then there was fanaticism. People demanded miracles. Padre Pio told these people that he was just a poor friar who prays. He said, "What can I do? Everything comes from God. I am rich in only one thing: infinite misery."

Segregation

The devil wasted no time sticking his tail in the midst of it all, and bitter conflicts and controversies erupted from within the order, the diocese of Manfredonia, and even in Rome. While many were convinced Padre Pio was a saint, some believed otherwise. They considered Padre Pio to be a charlatan, an Italian Rasputin, a fraud who faked his wounds to his own benefit. The result was jealousy, envy, and resentment leading to the worst forms of slander against Padre Pio. The bishop of Manfredonia, whose diocese included San Giovanni Rotondo, welcomed reports of Padre Pio and impropriety with women, which he promptly communicated to the Holy See.

One of the most consequential medical reports was penned by the illustrious Franciscan priest-doctor, Padre Agostino Gemelli. Not only was he the founder and first rector of the eminent Università Cattolica del Sacro Cuore (Catholic University of the Sacred Heart) in

Milan, he founded a teaching hospital in Rome. Today, the Agostino Gemelli Policlinico (known colloquially as the "Gemelli"), is the most important Italian hospital in the city of Rome.

After Padre Gemelli's brief visit to the sacristy of San Giovanni Rotondo (in which, under obedience, Padre Pio would not reveal his stigmata, since the visit was unscheduled and unapproved), he became one of Padre Pio's harshest critics. In his report to the Holy Office (the name was changed to the Congregation for the Doctrine of Faith in 1965), he wrote, "This is a case of suggestion unconsciously produced by Padre Benedetto in a sick subject such as Padre Pio and which has led to those characteristic manifestations of psittacism that are typical of the hysterical structure." His criticism was instrumental in the restrictive measures and censures that soon arrived.

In 1922, the Roman Curia intervened forcefully. The first investigation on behalf of the Holy Office declared Padre Pio's stigmata to be "not of supernatural origin." A decree was issued warning the faithful not to approach Padre Pio for reasons of devotion, and he was not permitted to show his hand to be kissed. It was recommended he celebrate Mass at contrasting times, preferably early in the morning.

Religious authorities began considering relocating Padre Pio to a different convent. However, once rumors began circulating regarding the imminent transfer of their "saint," the people of San Giovanni Rotondo – the *Sangiovannesi* – declared their intent to have him remain in their village by any means – even by armed uprising, if necessary. When an armed group of local militia began guarding the convent in day and night shifts, the authorities backed off. Such threats were taken seriously. They had reason to be. Not long before, the "Massacre of San Giovanni Rotondo" had taken place.

On the morning of October 14, 1920, the Socialist Party was celebrating their victory in a recent election by processing through the village with red flags and a musical band. When the throng stopped in the center of town with the intention of raising the red flag over City Hall, a group of counter protesters formed. Made up of carabinieri, veteran soldiers, and fascists, the two groups collided and shots rang out. In the aftermath, thirteen dead and eighty wounded were counted.

Throughout the period of Padre Pio's defamation, his supporters came to his defense with their own smear campaign. Emanuele Brunatto was a spiritual son and fierce defender of Padre Pio. He had had a powerful conversion after Padre Pio intervened in his life, and (remarkably) had been authorized to live in the convent for a period of time. Taking matters into his own hands, he began investigating the personal lives of the bishops and priests who were against Padre Pio. He initiated a media campaign in an attempt to cast favorable light on Padre Pio and to discredit those prelates who were opposed to him. Against the wishes of Padre Pio, he published a series of articles and books under a pseudonym, in which he highlighted alleged miracles and other extraordinary phenomena that were taking place in San Giovanni Rotondo and, at the same time, exposed the immorality of the prelates. His attempt at blackmail backfired.

Soon afterwards, the saga came to a head. On May 23, 1931, the Holy Office issued its decree: "Padre Pio da Pietrelcina is deprived of any exercise of ministry with the sole exception of celebrating Holy Mass, but inside the walls of the convent, in the chapel privately and not in public." The decree reached the friary in San Giovanni Rotondo on June 9. In his memoirs, the superior of San Giovanni Rotondo, Padre Raffaele da Sant'Elia a Pianisi, described Padre Pio's reaction when he handed him the order:

> After vespers, while Padre Pio was in the choir to pray as usual, I called him into the sitting room. He immediately came. I communicated to him the decree of the Holy Office, which prohibited him from celebrating in public and hearing the confessions of both the faithful and religious. Raising his eyes to heaven, he said: "May God's will be done!" Then he covered his eyes with his hands, bowed his head, and breathed no more. I tried to comfort him, but he found comfort only in Jesus hanging from the cross. Shortly after, he returned to the choir and remained there until midnight and longer.

The next two years were the darkest of Padre Pio's life. From that moment, Padre Pio was suspended from all priestly ministries, including celebrating Mass publicly, hearing confessions, communicating with the laity in person or via letters, and from giving blessings. Within the community, he was further prohibited from teaching or directing the students and from hearing their confessions. He could celebrate Mass, but only privately and in the presence of just one attendant. Padre Agostino wrote in his diary: "I was able to attend his Mass in the internal chapel. Whoever serves the Holy Mass closes the back door, so that no one can enter it. Thus Padre [Pio] scrupulously observes the order of the Holy Office."

The beginning of the end of his de facto imprisonment was on July 16, 1933. Due to a series of events (guided by the Holy Spirit), Pope Pius XI ordered a reversal of the ban on Padre Pio's public celebration of Mass, saying, "I have not been badly disposed toward Padre Pio, but I have been badly informed." Initially, Padre Pio was allowed only to hear confessions of the religious inside and outside the community. The following year, he was permitted to hear men's confessions and later still, the women's, but only in the morning. It wasn't until 1941 when the full faculties of his priestly ministries were reinstated.

Padre Pio was obedient, following the vows he professed. As a Capuchin dedicated to conformity to Christ Crucified, he could not have done otherwise. Just as Christ's obedience to the will of the Father led him to the cross, Pio's obedience led him to die to self in the exercise of his ministries.

Spiritual Sons and Daughters

From the time Padre Pio was ordained and living back in Pietrelcina for health reasons, groups of devoted followers began forming around him, particularly women. From the time he was reassigned to San Giovanni Rotondo, the faithful would trudge up to the friary daily to attend his long, early morning Mass and prayers. Others from out of town came to San Giovanni Rotondo and returned often. After his notoriety spread, he began meeting people of all backgrounds: poor and rich, men and women, noble and commoners, politicians, doctors and scientists, people of culture, the educated and illiterate.

Padre Pio grew close to his devotees and a unique spiritual friendship began blossoming. From these men and women, Padre Pio discerned and chose some of them to become even closer to him. They were known as his spiritual sons and daughters. These carefully chosen people were able to speak to him, go to him often for confession, ask for counsel, rely on his wisdom, and receive his prayers. He loved them as a father loves his sons and daughters.

Not everyone who asked to become a spiritual child was accepted. There are plenty of anecdotes to this end. There was a gentleman who confessed to Padre Pio, whom Padre did not believe had the proper contrition to receive absolution. Brazenly, the same man asked if he could become his spiritual child.

"No," he responded brusquely. "You are not even a child of God."

When he did accept someone, it often came with an admonition, "Yes, I accept you as my spiritual son (or daughter). However, do not make a bad impression." (Ita: *fare una brutta figura*.) He meant that the most important condition for being his spiritual child was to imitate his holy life and practice the virtues. Just as all children reflect certain characteristics of their earthly fathers, being a spiritual son or daughter of Padre Pio meant mirroring the spirituality of Padre Pio. It necessitated a commitment to the Christian life in a significant way. It meant striving to practice the virtues, to embrace a life of serious prayer, to make countercultural choices, and, in effect, to live the Gospel.

Padre Pio watched over his spiritual sons and daughters to the point that he considered their souls as his own. He used to say solemnly: "When the Lord entrusts me with a soul, I place it on my shoulders and I never give it up." He also said, in a powerful statement of devotion and true charity, "I can forget myself, but not my spiritual children. Indeed, I assure you that when the Lord calls me, I will say to him: 'Lord, let me stand at the threshold of heaven; I shall not enter until the last of my children enter.'"

Over the years, Padre Pio called on his spiritual sons and daughters to help him fulfill (prayerfully and practically) his spiritual, charitable, and apostolic works, including one of his most ambitious works – a hospital.

The Hospital

Padre Pio's desire to help the poor and suffering began in childhood. In recalling his youth, he once said: "The appearance of this hovel pained me so much that, taking half a lira, which I had in my pocket, I gave it to the poor man." As a priest, the desire to help the poor and suffering only increased. In a letter to Padre Benedetto, dated March 26, 1914, he wrote:

> Deep down in my soul, it seems to me, God has poured out many graces of compassion for the sufferings of others, especially with regard to the poor and needy. The immense pity I experience at the sight of a poor man gives rise deep down in my soul a most vehement desire to help him, and if I were to follow the dictates of my will I should be driven to strip myself even of clothing in order to cover him.
>
> When I know that a person is afflicted in soul or in body, what would I not do to have the Lord relieve him of his sufferings! Willingly would I take upon myself all his afflictions in order to see him saved, and I would even hand over to him the benefits of such sufferings if the Lord would allow it. (*Letters*, Vol. I, p. 519 - Edizioni Padre Pio da Pietrelcina, 2012)

The tremendous suffering endured by Padre Pio is clear. Much has already been made of his physical illnesses, psychological distress from scrupulosity, and spiritual bouts of diabolical vexation. Further, the coinciding of his desire to be a suffering servant, his priesthood, and the reception of the stigmata has also been recounted. The humiliations and persecutions he endured at the hands of his superiors and prelates only added to his sufferings. Due to all this, he carried within himself a profound sensitivity toward the suffering of others.

People came to him from all social classes begging him to intercede for them and their loved ones for an end to every form of illness and misery. While Padre Pio pined to eliminate their suffering, he had no power to effect miracles. Certainly, his ministry frequently led to consolation and countless spiritual healings. But physical healings did not depend on him. But all he could do was pray and offer his sufferings for the good of others. If a miracle was to be granted, it was because God willed it, not Padre Pio. He was merely the intercessor, not the author of any healing. He once said to a spiritual son who asked him to work a miracle for his dying father, "Life is good and is not ours. We are born naked and we die more naked still. If I could have, I would have saved my own mother [from death]. We must lower ourselves to the will of God."

In this context – and the fact that health care was limited in that milieu geographically and economically – his desire to aid the sick began to express itself in a concrete corporal work of mercy. What eventually became the extraordinary hospital complex that today dominates the skyline of San Giovanni Rotondo took time to realize. It was conceived in fits and starts.

The first attempt at a clinic was a collaboration between Padre Pio and the friars and a state program called "*Congregazione di Carità*" (Congregation of Charity). The result was a simple clinic inaugurated in 1925 on the premises of a former Poor Clare monastery in the old town of San Giovanni Rotondo. Named after St. Francis, it was called *Ospedale San Francesco* (St. Francis Hospital). It consisted of two wings, one for men and one for women, each with seven beds. Health care was free of charge for the poor and indigent. However, due to poor management, little by little it fell into disuse. An earthquake in 1938 put an end to the project. Though the St. Francis Hospital did not come to fruition, larger fruits were about to be borne. Padre Pio's desire to help the sick was stronger than ever.

The following year, a more ambitious project was launched. On January 9, 1940, Padre Pio spoke with a group of people consisting of some of his most trusted spiritual sons and daughters, in addition to doctors and entrepreneurs. He expressed his desire to create a center where the sick would feel at home and where patients could be healed in soul as well as body. It would be a comfortable place, full of light, and family-like. Not all of the early collaborators were experts, but they all shared in Padre's vision. When asked what the new clinic would be called, Padre Pio took a few days to respond. On January 14, he gave the definitive answer: "Home for Relief of Suffering" (Ita: *Casa Sollievo della Sofferenza*).

Instead of locating the new clinic in the center of town, it would be situated next to the friary and church. Maria Basilio, a spiritual daughter of Padre Pio, owned land adjacent to the sanctuary complex. According to the deed, it could only be used for works of charity. She agreed to donate the land to Padre Pio's project. And so it began.

No serious economist or businessperson would have recommended the construction of a hospital in such a location. Not only was it far from town, the site consisted of sloping, solid rock that would have to be cleared. Furthermore, the Gargano was one of the most economically depressed areas in the entire region of Puglia, and the roads and access in and out of San Giovanni Rotondo were inadequate. It made no sense. Yet, Padre Pio and the others were convinced. He was doing this work for one reason: the Relief of Suffering. Padre Pio believed it was God's work, and – as if daring God – they commenced.

It was not without setbacks. Initially, there were challenges mostly related to finances and labor. But the biggest obstacle was World War II. At the conclusion of the war, with a cash fund of only 4 million lire, construction began in earnest. On May 16, 1947, Padre Pio blessed the first stone of the Home for Relief of Suffering with the words: "We must thank Divine Providence who will allow us to carry out this great work for the good of humanity."

Angelo Lupi, from the region of Abruzzo, was neither an engineer nor a surveyor, but he was esteemed by Padre Pio. He began overseeing the project. Hundreds of veterans returning from the war were recruited to excavate and clear the hard Gargano rock. Many of them were unemployed, and they were overjoyed to work with Padre

Pio on the creation of such an opus. To everyone, it appeared as a gift of Providence, born of spirituality and charity. Once construction began, donations began flowing in from all over Italy and abroad. Generous gifts came from the United States, especially after English speaking journalists began reporting on the project.

After nine years, the *policlinico* (outpatient clinic) was inaugurated on May 5, 1956. Padre Pio considered it his greatest work, the "the apple of my eye." During the inauguration, presided over by Cardinal Giacomo Lercaro from Bologna, Padre Pio gave a riveting talk in which he outlined the work:

> A seed has been placed in the earth that He will warm with His rays of love. Do not deprive us of your help, collaborate in this apostolate of relief of human suffering. A first step of the journey to be taken has been made. Let us not stop our pace, let us respond promptly to God's call for the cause of good, each one fulfilling his duty: I, in unceasing prayer as a useless servant of our Lord Jesus Christ; you with the poignant desire to hold all suffering humanity to your heart to present it with me to the mercy of the heavenly Father.

The day after the inauguration, Padre Pio said to the doctors present: "You have the mission to cure the sick; but if you do not bring love to the sick bed, I do not think that medications are of much use. Bring God to the sick: it will be worth more than any other cure. In the sick, you treat Christ; in the sick who are poor, you treat Christ twice!" In these words, Padre Pio revealed his desire for the hospital. It was to be understood as a place where prayer and science were united – a collaboration between religion and medicine. Therefore, in addition to doctors, there had to be chaplains to minister to the patients.

At the behest of Padre Pio, sisters arrived from the Congregation of the Apostles of the Sacred Heart of Jesus. Founded with a mission dedicated to "bring together orphans, the poor and abandoned, and disadvantaged children," they shared Padre Pio's vision. Their ministries at the hospital would focus on the spiritual, psychological, and religious dimension, and they would accompany "the sick to establish, recover or intensify his or her relationship with God." Their activities were not limited to the patients, and they included the entire hospital community: doctors, nurses, officials, patients and relatives of the sick.

On the first anniversary of the opening, on May 5, 1957, Padre Pio summarized the work carried out the first year and mapped out his vision for the future. He spoke of a "hospital city equipped with the technology for the most audacious clinical needs." He hoped for "many more beds – two houses, one for women and one for men – where weary and tired spirits and bodies come to the Lord and are 'relieved' by him." He foresaw an "Intercontinental Study Center" for the improvement of professional culture and for the Christian formation of health care workers, so that the work would become more and more "a temple of prayer and science, where humanity finds itself in Jesus Crucified as a single sheepfold, under a single shepherd." In order for all these ambitious goals to be fulfilled, he knew he could not rely merely on the good will of the people. It would take prayer to carry it out.

Prayer Groups

While the hospital was being built, in parallel, groups of prayer began. The groups were a response to an appeal of the pope. At the conclusion of World War II, Pope Pius XII asked the faithful to gather together to pray for the strength to rebuild society, devastated by the scourge, materially and morally. He asked them to pray for peace, unity, and the salvation of the world. Padre Pio heard the pontiff's plea, and in 1949 began exhorting his spiritual sons and daughters and those who came to San Giovanni Rotondo to pray as the pope asked. Immediately, people throughout Italy and other European countries began forming in groups to pray according to the intentions of the pope and Padre Pio.

The groups maintained contact with San Giovanni Rotondo through a magazine that took its name from the hospital, "*La Casa Sollievo della Sofferenza.*" The official appeal for the establishment of formal Prayer Groups was published in the August 1950 issue. By the end of that year, there were already twenty-three officially registered groups. In later issues, Padre Pio would give guidelines and instructions about the hospital and its mission. Thus, the Prayer Groups were initially called on to spiritually accompany the mission of the Home for Relief of Suffering and, as such, were intimately connected to the works of the hospital.

With that, the first Padre Pio Prayer Groups were conceived. They were a spiritual movement of the laity, all over the world, whose fundamental charism was intercessory prayer. As they grew, Padre Pio asked priests to assume spiritual guidance over the Groups in such a way as to guarantee a bond with the Church.

On May 4, 1986, the Statutes of the Prayer Groups were formally approved by the Holy See. According to the Statutes, the Prayer Groups are based on three general principles inspired by the Franciscan spirituality of Padre Pio:

- Full adherence to the doctrine of the Catholic Church, led by the Pope and the Bishop;
- Prayer with the Church, for the Church and in the Church, participation in the liturgy and sacraments in communion with God;
- Charity intended for the care and relief of the suffering and the needy, as a concrete example of charity towards God.

The Charisms of Padre Pio

From the time of his childhood, Padre Pio was endowed with extraordinary, supernatural gifts, including visions of the spiritual world. It was as if the veil between the heavens and the earth had been lifted up for him permitting him to see what lay beyond the natural world. Even as a child, his intimacy with his Guardian Angel was such that he expressed dismay in learning that others did not see and hear angels as he did.

As he grew, so did the gifts. After he entered the order, in Sant'Elia a Pianisi, God began revealing to Pio ways in which he would be called to use these gifts. After ordination, the gifts grew in leaps and bounds. By the time the stigmata appeared and people began flocking to San Giovanni Rotondo, the strange phenomena they witnessed began to spread. It soon became clear that Padre Pio was the recipient of multiple charisms.

Charisma is the Greek word used by St. Paul in the New Testament meaning "favor," "gratuitous gift," or "benefit." Charisms are extraordinary, special graces given by the Holy Spirit to individuals to be used at the service of charity for the sanctification of others and to build up the Church. (See CCC 2003.)

The main charisms Padre Pio received from God include: (1) scrutiny of souls; (2) bilocation; (3) odor of sanctity; (3) prophecy; and (4) intercessory prayer.

Scrutiny of Souls

Padre Pio had the ability to look inside souls and see with the eyes of the Holy Spirit. There are countless testimonies of people who experienced this firsthand, especially in the sacrament of reconciliation. Cleonice Morcaldi, one of Padre Pio's earliest and closest spiritual daughters, once asked him how he could read her soul. He replied: "Through Jesus I see everything you do and everything you say. I see your soul as you see yourself in a mirror."

Due to this gift, Padre Pio knew how to treat penitents in the confessional. Most of the time, he comforted people as a loving, paternal father. However, when warranted, he would sometimes withhold absolution. He could see if a penitent had omitted sins, if the soul were truly contrite, or if that person were there out of curiosity or to test him. When he denied absolution, penitents would go away angry or distraught. Many times, they would repent and return, becoming his most fervent devotees and spiritual sons and daughters.

Bilocation

Bilocation is a rare charism in which a person appears physically in two places at the same time. The bilocating person can speak, listen, move, and otherwise interact with people. Though Padre Pio never left San Giovanni Rotondo after 1918, countless people testified to having seen him all over Italy, and beyond.

Padre Pio appeared in bilocation at the bedsides of dying people, in the confessional, or in other circumstances of need. The first documented episode of this gift has been recounted – when Padre Pio appeared at the birth of noblewoman, Giovanna Boschi, while her father was dying. One of the most remarkable circumstances of bilocation took place during World War II when Padre Pio appeared in a cloud before two American fighter pilots who were ordered to bomb San Giovanni Rotondo. After they saw his face, they turned back without dropping any bombs.

In 1921, Padre Pio was interrogated by Monsignor Raffaello Carlo Rossi, inquisitor of the Holy Office. Regarding bilocation, under oath, Padre Pio replied:

> I happened to be in the presence of this or that person, in this or that place. I don't know if my mind was transported there, or if what I saw was some sort of vision of the place or the person. Nor do I know if I was there with my body, or just with the spirit. For example, one evening I found myself at the bedside of a sick woman, Maria Massa, in San Giovanni Rotondo. I was in the convent. I think I was praying. I did not know her personally. She had been recommended to me.

Odor of Sanctity

Sometimes Padre Pio communicated to people from afar through perfume or fragrance. Known as the "odor of sanctity," people would suddenly and overwhelmingly smell a fragrance. He usually used it as a sign of his presence, usually to assist those suffering. While he often used it to aid his spiritual sons and daughters, sometimes people who had never had any contact with him experienced the odor of sanctity. The fragrance was usually that of roses, but it could be violets or lilies of the valley. When taking place, the smell was intense and unmistakable.

Sometimes, on the other hand, Padre Pio used unpleasant odors, like tobacco or carbolic acid. As he used sweet fragrances to console, he used foul odors to get people's attention. Sometimes, these people were in physical danger or were in the midst of a strong moral temptation. What is certain is that Padre Pio made his presence or assistance felt from a distance through perfumes and odors. (Note that here I have used the past tense, though Padre Pio continues to communicate to people today through the odor of sanctity.)

Prophecy

Another charism Padre Pio received was that of prophecy. Sometimes referred to as clairvoyance, prophecies relate to the foreknowledge of future events, though they may apply to past events or present, hidden things which cannot be known through reason or natural means. Such knowledge is supernaturally infused by God, as it concerns events or facts beyond the natural power of intelligence.

There are countless anecdotes of spiritual sons and daughters and those who confessed to or spoke with Padre Pio, even briefly, regarding how he saw a future event that eventually took place. Padre Pio used prophecy to help people understand God's will and to strengthen, encourage, and console, as well as to admonish.

Intercessory Prayer

One of Padre Pio's greatest charisms was that of intercessory prayer. Intercessory prayer is mystically linked to the salvific actions of Christ's Passion and Resurrection. By offering up one's own sufferings and prayers and uniting them to Christ's, one can aid in another's salvation.

Padre Pio constantly interceded for his spiritual children and for many who turned to him asking for his aid. This is one of the motives underlying his long Masses: at the moment of the elevation of the host and chalice, he prayed for each of his spiritual sons and daughters and the intentions of those who asked him for prayer.

He also used his frequent illnesses as forms of intercession. He often experienced high fevers (known as hyperthermia) that should have been lethal. The mercury would shoot up off the scale in household thermometers, so that the friars and doctors would have to use veterinary or bath thermometers. In his report to the Holy Office, Dr. Festa wrote that there were days in which Padre Pio's temperature would rise to 48° or 49° C (118° or 120° F). During such bouts, he would offer himself as a victim for those for whom he was interceding. Countless people have reported that they or their loved ones were healed in the same moment Padre Pio was offering himself in expiation for them through his high fevers and illnesses.

The Spirituality of Padre Pio

As the years and decades wore on in San Giovanni Rotondo, the Capuchin community settled into something resembling normalcy. The friars somehow managed to streamline and organize the arrival of pilgrims, cynics, fanatical devotees, and desperate cases. The extraordinary events his confreres witnessed on a daily basis became ordinary.

By now, Padre Pio had become a larger-than-life religious figure known throughout Italy and the Catholic Church at large. He was a household name. His relationship with the authorities of the Church eventually settled into a sort of truce. While not everyone seated in bishoprics or the Roman Curia was fond of him, they had no choice. Not only did he have an army of loyal supporters, the evangelical nature of what was happening in San Giovanni Rotondo could not be ignored. Innumerable people were coming to San Giovanni Rotondo and going away transformed. Many who came with doubts, stony hearts, and burdened with sin went away with hope, a new spirit, and redeemed. If one applied the Gospel to discern whether or not Padre Pio was a false prophet or a wolf in sheep's clothing, the unavoidable fact is that the fruits were superabundant. (See Matthew 7:15-20).

One of Padre Pio's final accusations was the result of microphones that had been planted by one of his confreres in the guesthouse and in his cell. A recording picked up one of his spiritual daughters kissing his hand and made it all the way to the apostolic palace in Rome. To his enemies, it was proof of illicit relations with women. But to the priest who understood the beatitude, it was a spiritual benefit: "Blessed are you when they insult you and persecute you and utter every kind of evil against you [falsely] because of me" (Matthew 5:11).

Il Padre ("the Father" as he was referred to affectionately by those who knew him) remained unfazed by all the commotion and continued his mission of saving sinners and healing the sick. He arose each day at 3:30 AM, and went down to the church to prepare spiritually for Mass, which began at 5:00. Crowds of the faithful arrived early to ensure a place to sit. He celebrated on the main altar in the nave, as well as a side altar in the right aisle dedicated to St. Francis. After Mass, *il Padre* would spend most of the rest of the day hearing confessions. His primary ministries – Mass and Reconciliation – would be interrupted only for meals (during which he usually fasted), a brief period of rest after lunch, and meetings – scheduled or impromptu – with friars, spiritual sons and daughters, and those from out of town who had appointments to meet him.

Despite his packed days, he managed to spend a remarkable amount of time in prayer. In addition to his long morning Mass and the fixed prayers of the divine office, he also prayed before the Blessed Sacrament and devoted time to mental prayer. But his main "weapon" was the rosary. He prayed multiple rosaries throughout the day. Those who knew him recount that he kept his rosary within his pocket which he constantly fingered while mouthing Paters, Aves, and Glorias. He referred to the rosary as the "sweet chain that binds us to God;" "the best weapon to defend oneself from the snares of the evil one;" and the "key that opens the Heart of God."

If what has been written thus far describes external aspects of Padre Pio, what is more pertinent is what was taking place within. And this is much more difficult to convey. There is a reason so many people flocked to Padre Pio. Within him, they saw Jesus or, more properly, they experienced Christ. Merely being in the presence of Padre Pio was powerful. It changed people's lives.

Adolfo Affatato, one of the last living spiritual sons of Padre Pio wrote about what it was like to be in the presence of Padre Pio:

During his long silences, punctuated only by the movement of his fingers on rosary beads, the spiritual delight was amazing. An energetic strength charged with heavenly presence within him emanated from his persona. I cannot express what I felt in those moments as every word is inadequate to describe the boundless joy that overflowed from my heart.

During those times, my mind was emptied of every thought and concern. My body was calm and relaxed and I had complete control over my senses and feelings. I felt lightness and a joy that pervaded my entire self. I felt well, very well.

When you experience something like this – involving all your emotions – you never want it to end. Only those who have felt this know what I mean. Only those who had the good fortune to experience such events personally can have a more realistic picture of who Padre was than those who would write about him after historical studies.

Padre Pio's entire life was a living and concrete demonstration of the presence of Christ within through his living crucified body, a source of miracles, through which God in His mercy poured out His love on humanity. This love was nothing other than the same love Padre Pio had toward God, which the Most High reciprocated by working miracles for numerous souls who were grasping in the dark. The intense love of God was manifested through an intense heat of the heart, an intense burning heat of the heart – a true fire of love. Padre Pio himself once wrote: "I feel my heart and insides completely absorbed by the flames of a great fire that grows ever larger. I am a volcano that is always aglow."

The figure of Padre Pio is so grand and enlightened that my words are likely of little use. To speak of Padre Pio would take another Padre Pio, or a Saint Francis, or the voice of God Himself. So how can one transmit the idea of who this great saint was? This saint who illuminated the darkness of the twentieth century with his presence? Through the episodes experienced by those who had the privilege of being close to him when he walked among us. This is up to his spiritual children, which I am one of the last — a living witness to and recipient of extraordinary events that the human mind cannot comprehend.

This is a snapshot of what those blessed, fortunate souls experienced in the presence of Padre Pio.

The Final Years

As Padre Pio's popularity grew, houses began going up in the area closer to the sanctuary and medical complex. In addition to the *Sangiovannesi*, who wanted to be closer to Padre Pio, homes were built for doctors and hospital staff who had relocated to town as the hospital expanded. Others still came from out of town also desiring to be close to their spiritual father. Some relocated permanently, while others wanted their own place to stay for frequent visits.

Then there were the pilgrims and the faithful who came by busloads. As the crowds increased, so did the infrastructure. The dirt roads around the village were paved and enlarged. Further out, state highways and provincial roads were built or improved to better connect San Giovanni Rotondo with the cities of San Severo, Manfredonia, and Foggia. Locally, hotels, inns, souvenir shops, and restaurants began lining the road between the old town and the sanctuary and hospital. All were necessary to serve the crowds who needed to eat, sleep, and bring home a souvenir of their visit.

It didn't take long before Padre Pio outgrew the ancient church. Built in the sixteenth century as a hermitage and wayside votive shrine for the shepherds and penitent souls who ventured up the mountain, it had become woefully inadequate to accommodate the hordes in the era of Padre Pio. In 1952, the Minister General of the Capuchin Order, Padre Benigno da Sant'Ilario Milanese, proposed the construction of a new, larger church. In the meantime, he petitioned the Holy Office to allow Padre Pio to celebrate Mass outdoors, under the portico, on days when there was a large turnout. Two years later, he obtained the *nulla osta* from Rome, and Padre Pio began celebrating outside. At the same time, he received authorization to enlarge the current church. In January 1955, while the hospital was being completed, construction on the new church began just a few meters away. On July 2, 1956, the first stone was laid, and three years later, on July 1, 1959, the new church of Santa Maria delle Grazie was consecrated.

As Padre Pio aged and was constantly pained by his stigmata and other sufferings, his desire to aid the poor and suffering never wavered. One of his final works of charity was aimed at helping young people find work. While the construction and operation of the hospital created some jobs, unemployment was still staggeringly high. When an indigent man around the age of twenty came out to the friary begging in early 1957, Padre Pio had an idea: a center to instruct young men in the professional trades. With that, a vocational training center was conceived. Called "St. Joseph the Artisan," it was inaugurated on January 26, 1958 and was the first of its kind in the region. Under the leadership of the Tertiaries (Secular Franciscans) and a priest, it soon transformed hundreds of unemployed young men into skilled workers.

On April 25, 1959 Padre Pio fell ill. From that time until August 8, he celebrated Mass in the internal chapel. During that period, he began the custom of greeting the faithful from the convent window for the noontime Angelus prayer. When his spiritual sons and daughters saw how aged and feeble he appeared, they began to ask themselves the unthinkable. What would they do when he was gone?

15: The Death and Glorification of St. Pio of Pietrelcina

When the Second Vatican Council began on October 11, 1962, Padre Pio was seventy-five years old. Many prelates and theologians in Italy for the council journeyed down to Puglia to meet the famed friar for themselves. They were struck by the saintly Capuchin whose demeanor was signed by decades of illness and suffering. When he moved, he shuffled about visibly pained, especially due to the marks on his feet. The wounds had never ceased causing him distress. His most devoted spiritual daughters and sons wept out of compassion at the moving sight.

His vision was becoming more impaired, and he was authorized to pray the rosary instead of the divine office. He continued to celebrate the Mass in Latin, by now through rote memory. In March, 1968, he could no longer feel his legs, and he moved about with the aid of a wheelchair. He then obtained permission to remain seated while celebrating Mass. On some days, he was unable to officiate in the church, and he celebrated in the convent chapel. Sometimes he was not even able to leave his cell. On July 7, he had a severe fall. He recovered, but from that moment onward, he withdrew more and spoke little. It was the beginning of the end.

On September 20, 1968, San Giovanni Rotondo was bustling with activity. Members of the Prayer Groups, spiritual sons and daughters, and other devotees of Padre Pio had come from all over the world. They were there to commemorate the fiftieth anniversary of Pio's stigmatization. It was the first international meeting of the Prayer Groups, which were set to receive official recognition by the Holy See the following day.

Padre Pio celebrated Mass on September 20, but with difficulty. The next day he did not come down. He had had an asthma attack and was unable to leave his cell. That evening, he managed to participate in the vespers and bless the immense crowd.

On September 22, he celebrated Mass at 5:00 AM, but again with difficulty. He almost fainted due to low blood pressure, and his confreres had to take him into the sacristy where he recovered. He kept saying over and over, "My children, my children!" Afterwards, he tried to hear confessions, but was unable and he returned to his cell. His confreres recognized that something was different. That night, before retiring to his bed, he managed to greet the crowd from his window and wave his white handkerchief. This was his last appearance in public.

Padre Pellegrino Funicelli was tasked with looking after him that night. He wrote a touching account of what he witnessed early on the morning of September 23. It was published in a special edition in the magazine, *The House for Relief of Suffering*, with the title, "Padre Pio has died":

> Shortly after 9:00 PM on September 22, 1968, when Padre Mariano finished his turn, he left cell no. 4, and I entered. Padre Pio called me into his room through the intercom. He was in bed, lying on his right side. He asked me the time on the alarm clock on his bedside table. I wiped away some tears from his reddened eyes and went back to cell no. 4 and continued monitoring the intercom.
>
> *Il Padre* called me another five or six times until midnight. His eyes were continuously red with tears, but it was a sweet, serene cry. At midnight, like a frightened child, he begged me: "Stay with me, my son." And he continuously asked me the time.

He looked at me with eyes full of pleading, while squeezing my hands tightly. Then, as if he had forgotten the time which he kept asking me, he asked: "Did you say Mass?"

Smiling, I replied: "Spiritual Father, it is too early now for Mass."

"Well, you're going to say it for me this morning," he said.

"Every morning I say it according to your intentions," I responded.

Then he wanted to confess. Once he had finished his sacramental confession, he said: "My son, if the Lord calls me today, ask the brothers for forgiveness for all the trouble I have caused them, and ask them and the spiritual children for a prayer for my soul."

I answered: "Spiritual Father, I am sure that the Lord will allow you to continue to live for a long time. But if you are right, can I ask you for one last blessing for the confreres, for your spiritual children, and for your sick ones?"

"Yes, I bless them all. On the contrary, ask the superior to give me this last blessing." Finally, he asked me to renew the act of religious profession.

At 1:00 AM, he said to me, "Listen, my son, I cannot breathe well here in bed. Let me get up. In my armchair I will breathe better."

Usually, he would get up at 1:00, 2:00, or 3:00 AM to prepare for Holy Mass, and before sitting down in the armchair he would walk along the corridor. That night I was amazed to see that he walked straight and briskly like a young man, so much so that he had no need of aid. When he reached the door of his cell, he said: "Let's go to the terrace for a bit."

I followed him, keeping my hand under his arm. He turned on the light himself and once he arrived at the armchair, he sat down and looked around the terrace curiously. He seemed to be searching for something with his eyes. After five minutes he wanted to go back to his cell. I tried to help him up, and he said, "I can't do it." In fact, he had grown heavy.

"Spiritual Father, do not worry," I told him encouraging him. I immediately got his wheelchair that was nearby. I lifted him out of the armchair beneath his arms and set him down in the wheelchair. He lifted his feet off the ground by himself and placed them on the footboard. When I had repositioned him in the armchair in his cell, he pointed at me with his left hand and looked at the wheelchair and said: "Take it out."

After I came back into the cell, I noticed that *il Padre* was beginning to turn pale and there was cold sweat on his forehead. I became frightened when I saw his lips starting to quiver. He continually repeated: "Jesus, Mary" with an ever weaker voice.

I started to go and call one of the confreres, but he stopped me, saying: "Do not wake anyone." I started off anyway and when I had walked a few steps from his cell, he called me again. And thinking that he hadn't called me back to say the same thing, I returned. But when he repeated himself saying: "Do not wake anyone," I replied with a plea: "Spiritual Father, let me do it now."

I rushed towards Padre Mariano's cell, but seeing Fra' Guglielmo's door open, I went in, turned on the light, and shook him saying, "Padre Pio is sick." Fra' Guglielmo rushed to *il Padre's* cell, and I ran to phone Dr. Sala. He arrived in about ten minutes and as soon as he saw *il Padre*, he began immediately preparing to give him an injection. When everything was ready, Fra' Guglielmo and I tried to lift him, but we could not, so we had to lay him on the bed. The doctor gave him the injection and then helped us put him back in the armchair. All the while, *il Padre* repeated in an increasingly faint voice and with the movement of his lips more and more imperceptibly: "Jesus, Mary."

Meanwhile, Dr. Sala called Mario Pennelli, Padre Pio's nephew; the medical director of the Casa Sollievo, Dr. Gusso; and Dr. Giovanni Scarale; while I called the Padre Guardian, Padre Mariano, and other confreres.

While the doctors gave him oxygen first with the cannister and then with the mask, Padre Paolo da San Giovanni Rotondo administered the Sacrament of the sick to our spiritual Father, and the other brothers kneeling around began praying.

At about 2:30, he gently bowed his head to his chest. He expired.

(Translated and printed with permission: La Casa Sollievo della Sofferenza, "*Padre Pio è morto*", October 1968)

Padre Pio was eighty-one years old, and had received the stigmata exactly fifty years earlier.

The friars prepared Padre Pio's body for burial. They placed a stole on his shoulders and a crucifix, rosary, and the Franciscan Rule in his hands. Dr. Sala removed his gloves and socks. To his amazement, he noted the stigmata had completely disappeared and there was no scarring. His flesh was healed. Those present who knew and understood Padre Pio and the mission given to him by God read the phenomenon through the eyes of faith. They understood that

Padre Pio's earthly mission was over. His wounds were of no more use. He was glorified now.

At 8:00 AM on September 26, Padre Pio's body was placed for viewing in the basilica of Santa Maria delle Grazie. The faithful waited as much as six hours to process through the church and view his body. At 3:30 PM, his remains were led in procession down to the old city of San Giovanni Rotondo. The cortege stopped at city hall where the mayor venerated his friend.

The funeral Mass began at 7:00 PM in Santa Maria degli Angeli. It was presided over by the Minister General of the Capuchin Order, Padre Clementinus von Vlissingen, while twenty-three priests concelebrated. At the end of the homily, a telegram sent by the Holy Father, Pope Paul VI, was read. Authorities estimated that 100,000 people were present in San Giovanni Rotondo that day.

At 8:30 PM, Padre Pio's remains were processed through the hospital of the Home for Relief of Suffering and then brought back to the church of Santa Maria delle Grazie. Then the door was closed. After the appropriate ecclesiastical seals were affixed to his coffin, his remains were carried down to the crypt and lowered into the niche that had been dug in the center of the room. The burial was complete by 10:00 PM.

The process of Padre Pio's beatification began one year after his death. Due to the many declared enemies of Padre Pio, there were numerous obstacles. After piles of documentation and paperwork was examined in Rome, on November 29, 1982, the *Nihil Obstat* was declared, and the following year, on March 20, 1983, the diocesan process for the canonization of the Servant of God Padre Pio was launched. On January 21, 1990 Padre Pio was proclaimed Venerable by Pope John Paul II, while the same pope declared him Blessed on May 2, 1999.

Though there were numerous miracles attributed to him, the miracle approved for his canonization involved a seven-year-old boy named Matteo Pio Colella from San Giovanni Rotondo. He was diagnosed with bacterial meningitis and his mother admitted him to the Casa Sollievo. His situation worsened and he was placed in an induced coma. He nearly went into cardiac arrest, and nine organs were seriously damaged. His parents then initiated a prayer chain to the intercession of Padre Pio. Little Matteo had a vision of Padre Pio, which he recounted once he came out of the coma.

"During my sleep, I was not alone; I saw an old man. I saw myself from afar, in this bed, through a round hole. I was near the machines, and an old man with a white beard and a long brown tunic gave me his right hand and said: 'Matteo, do not worry, you will soon be well.' And he smiled at me."

Matteo made a complete recovery. The Medical Council of the Congregation for the Causes of Saints declared on November 22, 2001: "The healing – rapid, complete and lasting, without sequelae – was scientifically inexplicable."

With this miracle, Padre Pio was proclaimed a saint. On June 16, 2002 in St. Peter's Square, Pope John Paul II presided over the canonization, just as he had the beatification. St. Pio's feast was set for September 23, the anniversary of his death.

Pope John Paul II – whose devotion to St. Pio of Pietrelcina is well known – addressed the new saint with the following words:

> Teach us, too, we beseech you, humility of heart, to be counted among the little ones of the Gospel, to whom the Father promised to reveal the mysteries of his Kingdom. Help us to pray without ever tiring, certain that God knows what we need, even before we ask for it. Obtain for us a glance of faith capable of readily recognizing the very face of Jesus in the poor and suffering. Support us in the hour of combat and trial and, if we fall, let us experience the joy of the sacrament of forgiveness. Transmit to us your tender devotion toward Mary, Mother of Jesus and of us. Accompany us on the earthly pilgrimage to the blessed Homeland, where we, too, hope to reach in order to contemplate eternally the Glory of the Father, the Son, and the Holy Spirit. Amen!

In the Footsteps, Part II

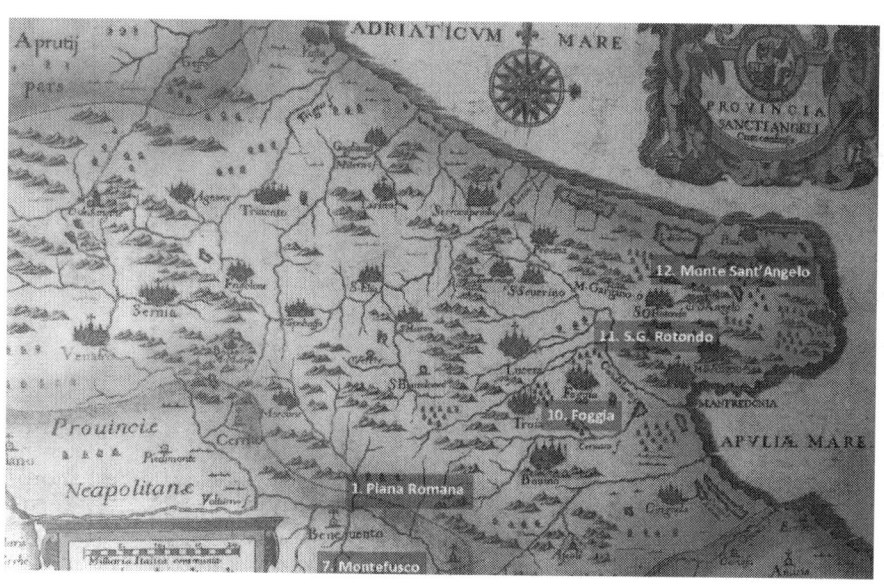

16: In the Footsteps: Piana Romana

Today we return to Pietrelcina, where we have one last site to visit: Piana Romana. This is the most poignant site in Padre Pio's native village, due to what took place there. We leave the old town with its rocky *murgia* and Houses of Padre Pio and set out to the countryside. We could drive 3.5 kilometers (2 mi), but we are going to take a different route: a walking path. It is known as the Via del Rosario (Rosary Way), though it is lined with the stations of the cross. This is the same route Padre Pio walked, as it is the shortest, most direct route from the Castle district to the property his parents owned.

As we head to the old part of town, I ask a gentleman working in a souvenir shop where the trail begins. He tells me to go toward the Houses of Padre Pio, then turn left, and "go down." I do as I'm told. As confirmation, just before the Madonnella door, an arrow points to the left indicating the Via del Rosario. I turn left, descend a few stairs, and then have a choice. I can go left again toward the *"bagni"* ("restrooms" indicated by a sign) or go right and descend a long flight of stone steps overgrown with vegetation. Though my intuition tells me to go left, I go right. It looks more interesting. I decide not to open up my GPS yet, though a hunch tells me I will need to do so soon.

As we descend, I think to myself that we are either going the wrong direction or no one has trodden the Rosary Way for a long time. The steps – well shaded by a canopy of trees and the *murgia* cliff of Pietrelcina to our right (and south) – are covered in moss and natural debris. It appears these steps get no sun. Nevertheless, I decide to continue. After we have descended at least 100 steps, we level out on a wide, flagstone pathway. Like the staircase, apparently no one has walked here for a long time, either. This is unfortunate, I think to myself as I consider the immense investment in treasure and labor it must have taken to create such a walkway. I look up to my right and see the cliff, the famed *murgia*, below the church of Sant'Anna.

After I am positive we are headed in the wrong direction, I break out my GPS and confirm that we are indeed not going in the direction of Piana Romana. We are going southwest, while the Forgione farm is to the northwest. I make a mental note: At the bottom of the *murgia*, go left, not right!

After we climb the 100 steps we just descended, I find the beginning of the trail – just by the restrooms indicated before the Madonnella door. It is just beneath the main parking lot of Pietrelcina and the square of St. John Paul II. It is well-marked and begins with a freshly laid flagstone path. This trail has obviously been walked on. It descends to a bridge over a creek that snakes around the old town of Pietrelcina, and then continues back uphill. I am impressed at the investment of the lengthy, recently constructed flagstone walkway. After the third station of the cross, however, the new path ends and an older stony road begins. This path is in much worse condition. I wonder if these are the original stones Padre Pio and his father walked along on their multitudinous trips back and forth into town.

The route to the Piana Romana is not long – "a solid thirty minutes," according to the shopkeeper back in Pietrelcina. As we get farther from town and deeper into farmland, I consider how pleasant it feels to be out here in the countryside. Though the trinket stands and souvenir shops are not excessive and they are an essential aspect of any pilgrimage destination, something feels more genuine out here. I look all around. This is the land Padre Pio walked on. These are the sights he saw. These are the scents he smelled. These are the sounds he heard. It is easy to imagine Francesco Forgione, or a young Padre

Pio, coming and going, as he walked among the oak trees and pines, the butterflies and bees, the barking dogs and singing birds, the smell of wood burning stoves and wild herbs. What a lovely area.

After about twenty minutes of gentle climbs and descents, I note how the area is still agrarian. I see so many small gardens and scattered farmhouses. Some have recently been renovated, while others are in ruins. The restored ones are probably used as summer homes, while the ruined ones may have been in working condition when Padre Pio was walking this pathway. Just outside one of the farmhouses in the distance, a woman is washing three olive oil drums, readying them for the approaching olive harvest and fresh oil. We pass a large field currently being ploughed by a farmer on a modern tractor. I notice what look like cornstalks and husks on the ground. It is maize, a heavy corn used for animal feed. I cannot help but notice how rich the soil is. It's almost black. While most of the scents in the air are pleasant, the manure is not.

After we come to a more developed area with larger tracts of farmland, I begin to see a large cross on the horizon in the distance. This is the area of Piana Romana. As we climb the final stretch up to Padre Pio's family farm, I turn around and look to the southwest and am struck by two prominent mountain ranges. They are the national parks of Taburno Camposauro and Partenio and are midway between Benevento and Naples. What a sight. The larger one to the right, the Taburno Camposauro, is in the shape of a sleeping woman – referred to as *la dormiente*, a woman lying supine on her back looking up.

As we follow Viale Padre Pio, flanked by small billboards for restaurants and B&Bs, we pass a working farm on the right. Finally, we arrive at the Piana Romana. A welcome sign invites visitors to explore the *masseria*, well, elm tree, and seat. The *masseria* – the small farmhouse owned by Zio Orazio – marks the beginning of the sites. A plaque in four languages describes it. The English inscription says:

> It has only a poor stone room, without plaster, or floor, with a fireplace and a mezzanine that served as a hay loft. Here on the farmyard the young Francesco (Padre Pio) met brother Camillo from Sant'Elia a Pianisi, a young Capuchin who was

begging, coming from the near friary of Morcone, seat for the novices from Foggia. It was this encounter that aroused in Francesco the wish to become "a monk with a beard," a Capuchin.

I enter the farmhouse and look beyond the protective, plastic barrier. It is one large room with a loft. As elsewhere, the room is comprised of vintage artefacts from the nineteenth century: a narrow bed, pictures of Padre Pio and his parents on the wall, recessed shelving with jugs, wooden chairs and desks, farm tools, household wares, a cross, and some icons. The flooring is made of rough-hewn stone and is original. In the far part of the room is a loft that was used for storing hay.

Behind the *masseria*, we follow a walkway hemmed in by rows of unmanicured olive trees on either side. In a few yards, we arrive at an old well equipped with a hoisted tin bucket. A metal cover has been inserted to plug up the opening. According to the legends, when Padre Pio was a boy, his father was irritated at not being able to find water. Young Francesco told his father to dig at this site. After a few days, he discovered water abundantly. There is a metal lever to pump the water. I try to move it, but it has been secured shut.

We continue a few more steps toward the chapel at the end of the walkway. Before entering, I walk behind it. There is a wrought iron fence enclosing some tall rocks deeply embedded into the ground. These were known as Padre Pio's "*seggioloni*" or "tall chairs." Padre Pio would sit on these rocks for prayer and reflection. He once said: "They were my high chairs. From there I watched the rising and setting of the sun."

We return and enter the chapel. This is the most important site in the Piana Romana. Behind a protective plastic wall is a simple space with a statue of Padre Pio kneeling. Behind him is a stump (what is left of the elm tree) and to his right a crucifix. Above the scene are words from Scripture: "I have been crucified with Christ." On the statue's hands and feet are the wounds of Christ. Here on September 7, 1910, Padre Pio received the stigmata for the first time. After he showed his hands to the parish priest, the two prayed that the wounds would disappear. They did, though the pain remained.

Before we leave, I spend a long time in prayer here. I consider what Padre Pio's life meant, why God willed these wounds to happen, and what they mean today. I ask myself questions that are impossible to answer, such as why God chose Padre Pio for these extraordinary gifts. I wonder if it was due to his humility and his deep surrender to Christ. We will never know, as God's ways are a mystery. "For my thoughts are not your thoughts, nor are your ways my ways—oracle of the LORD. For as the heavens are higher than the earth, so are my ways higher than your ways, my thoughts higher than your thoughts" (Isaiah 55:8-9).

I step outside the chapel, look around, and smile. Still largely untouched by modern life, this area has maintained its rustic charm as in the days of Padre Pio. It is not difficult to imagine young Francesco Forgione out here helping his parents tend to the fields and grazing flocks of sheep. Nor is it difficult to imagine a bearded Capuchin friar coming over the hill to ask for alms. I take in a breath of fresh air. Surely this air helped Padre Pio and his lungs.

We leave Piana Romana and return to Pietrelcina. There is still one more visit here: the church of the Holy Family and the Padre Pio Museum. After returning on the Rosary Way, we cross the bridge over the stream, head back up the stone staircase, and arrive at a small square dedicated to St. Pope John Paul II. Instead of turning left toward the Castello district and the Homes of Padre Pio, we continue straight. At the large parking lot, we turn left downhill toward the parish church of St. Mary of the Angels, then go right toward the more modern Gregaria district (now Viale Cappuccini). In a short distance, on the right, directly across from an elementary school, is the Capuchin convent and church of the Holy Family.

Unlike the other Capuchin convents and churches we have visited, this one is modern. It was built during Padre Pio's lifetime following his expressed wish. It is said that when he returned to Pietrelcina for health reasons, he was on an evening stroll towards the cemetery with the parish priest, Don Salvatore Pannullo, when he heard a "choir of angels singing and bells that pealed out fully." In the exact spot where he heard the bells, the Capuchin church and adjacent friary now stand.

Construction was financed by the American benefactress, Mary Pyle. Begun in 1926, the church was finished two years later, while the convent and entire complex was completed two decades later. The friars arrived in 1947, and four years later, it was consecrated by the archbishop of Benevento.

Constructed in neo-Romanesque style, the church is pleasant to visit. The interior consists of one nave and two side aisles. The central nave is wider than the aisles and is surmounted by a cross vault while the aisles are covered by a barrel vault. Along the side aisles are several altars with wooden sculptures and mosaics from the Vatican school. In the rear of the nave is the tomb of Padre Modestino da Pietrelcina (1917-2011).

Not being familiar with his life, I look up his story. I see that his cause of beatification and canonization was officially launched on September 14, 2020. Born in Pietrelcina, his mother was the same age as Francesco Forgione and she grew up near him and also tended sheep in the countryside of Piana Romana. Fra' Modestino became a spiritual son of Padre Pio and for forty-two years, he tirelessly carried out the service as porter of the convent of San Giovanni Rotondo.

Next to the church is a museum housing relics and objects related to the life of St. Padre Pio. It is much more extensive than the ones in the convents where he lived. The collection includes the actual cradle his mother rocked him in when he was a baby (it was donated by his family). There is the desk of his teacher, Angelo Caccavo, and notebook young Francesco used for his school work. As elsewhere, there are liturgical vestments, including stoles and albs, and vessels such as chalices, patens, and purifiers. There are also a pair of shoes and gloves. One of the more striking items is an alb that bears the marks of the stigmata of the flagellation.

With that, I make my way back to my B&B in the center of town. As we finish our excursion and I begin to pack my bags, I feel an immense sense of gratitude. A word comes to mind: gift. I have been gifted with an extraordinary experience here. I have walked in the footsteps of Padre Pio in his native town and have felt his accompaniment all along the way. Pietrelcina is a special place. I will remember it forever.

17: In the Footsteps: Montefusco and Foggia

This morning, after I say my *Addio*, my goodbye, I prepare for the day. I plan on visiting Montefusco on the way to Foggia before we head up to San Giovanni Rotondo. I am enthusiastic about our first visit, which includes a meeting with Fra' Raffaele Armiento, a friar stationed there. I met him some years ago when he was assigned to San Giovanni Rotondo. He is a young brother, in love with the Lord, and passionately devoted to Padre Pio. In retrospect, as I prepared for what should have been an uneventful day, I was blissfully unaware of the troubles and harrowing moments that awaited me.

Before leaving Pietrelcina, I check my GPS for the nearest methane gas station. My vehicle is known as an "exclusive" methane vehicle, which means it is manufactured to run exclusively on methane gas. (This allows for certain tax benefits.) It has a small, 15-liter (3.5 gallons) reserve tank of unleaded fuel designed solely to get to a methane station once the methane runs out. Until one year ago, methane gas was very inexpensive in Italy. But since the Russian invasion of Ukraine, natural gas has increased fivefold (yes, 500%!). Some stations, however, have hedged contracts with gas providers leading to wild price differences. Within a few kilometers of one another, price differences can be dramatic.

In fact, I check my CNG (Compressed Natural Gas) app, which indicates that there are two methane stations in Benevento. One sells methane at only €1.39 per unit, while the other offers it at €4.99 per unit. That's an easy decision and I opt for the first. I load the address into my GPS and am delighted to discover that it is close. Though the route will take me on back roads through the countryside, it is only fifteen minutes away. Perfect.

As we make our way out of Pietrelcina faithfully following the computer-generated route, the initial, paved *contrada* country road soon changes. After a few kilometers, it becomes an unpleasant semi-paved road, then hardly paved, then mostly a dirt road, until it is eventually little more than a mule track with intermittent piles of trash on either side. When it directs me to continue straight into what looks like a lake at the bottom of a hill, I turn back.

After a few more misunderstandings – I blame the GPS, though some might say it's the fault of the operator – I eventually arrive at the coveted methane station. I am happy to be here, because I have very little methane left, though my reserve tank of unleaded gas is almost full. As I make my final turn, I glance to my left and to my horror see a line of parked cars extending as far as the eye can see. I pull alongside a motorist who is in line for fuel and standing outside his vehicle smoking a cigarette engrossed in deep conversation with the driver behind him.

"How long is the wait?"

The standing motorist says one hour, while the seated guy adds thirty minutes to that. I shake my head, open my app, and double-check the other methane stations in the area. My only other choice is the one selling gas at €4.99 per unit. Not everyone locked into forward contracts before the Russian invasion. I shake my head and enter Montefusco into my GPS. I'll deal with fuel later.

When I have nearly arrived at the center of Montefusco, I vaguely recall Padre Emidio from Gesualdo telling me that the Capuchin convent is not in town, but is located about five kilometers (3 mi) out of town. So I pull over and now enter "cappuccini convento Montefusco." To my dismay, the new route tells me to turn back and drive seventeen minutes in another direction. I sigh and turn around. After a few more minutes twisting around more country roads, I begin to consider how much wear I have been inflicting on my tires the past few days.

After making my way up into the outskirts of town, my GPS finally tells me we are at our destination. I pull up alongside a lovely church. However, I have a sinking feeling we are not in Montefusco. There is nothing Capuchin- or Padre Pio-related anywhere. There are three gentlemen standing in front of the church. I ask one of them if this is the Capuchin convent.

"*Che?*" (What?), he asks with a bewildered look on his face.

"*I cappuccini.*"

"You mean Sant'Egidio… in Montefusco?"

"I think so."

"You're in Montemiletto. This is the church of Sant'Anna. Why did you come here?"

"I have no idea. The GPS told me to."

He nods his head in solidarity with my plight and gives me directions to Sant'Egidio in Montefusco, Italian style: "Go that way. [He points.] At the first roundabout, go left, then at the next intersection, go downhill, then right again and keep going downhill. You'll see the sign to Montefusco, follow it uphill. Then you'll see the church on your right. You can't get lost."

Confident I will get lost, I ignore his instructions, look up the address of Sant'Egidio Montefusco online directly on the Capuchin Province's website, copy it, and paste it into my GPS. I discover that I am, once again, another fifteen minutes away. More sighing.

By the time I finally get to my real destination — arriving about ninety minutes after I left Pietrelcina — I pull into the parking lot. I know I am in the right spot because there are four Capuchin friars standing outside in front of the church. As I pull into the parking lot, I wave. One of them looks at his wristwatch.

I secure my vehicle and walk toward the friars. Fra' Raffaele welcomes me to Montefusco with an embrace and asks why I'm so late. I tell him I left Pietrelcina about ninety minutes ago and recount my saga. With a bewildered look on his face, he asks why it took so long. He brings me to the edge of the parking lot and points to Pietrelcina in the distance.

"Look there," he says as he points to the north. "You can see the bell tower of Santa Maria degli Angeli." I don't look. I don't want to see. I want to forget.

I push the morning debacle out of my mind and turn my attention to the visit at hand. The church and convent of Sant'Egidio are about five or six kilometers (3-4 mi) from Montefusco in the distance. Again, while it was once out in the countryside, it has been encroached by sprawl. I look up at the exterior, which is made of red brick. This is the first brick exterior in any church I have seen. The convent, which extends in an L-shape to the right, is stuccoed and painted white. As elsewhere, it is a pleasant sight.

Fra' Raffaele helps me unwind and invites me in for an espresso. I accept. (Over many years of consuming the caffeinated beverage in Italy, it now has a sedative effect on me.) After some fellowship in the break room, Fra' Raffaele brings me into the church where I learn about the history of the Capuchins in Montefusco. The church was originally consecrated and inaugurated into the Capuchin Order on October 4, 1683. Like Gesualdo, it was once part of the Province of Naples. But in 1867, it was suppressed under the subversive laws of the Italian Kingdom. Then, on November 5, 1900, it was reacquired from the Italian Kingdom and integrated into this Province. Padre Pio da Benvenuto – the same Provincial Minister who worked to acquire the church and convent of Gesualdo for this Province – was behind the acquisition. In the past, it served as the theologate for the friars in formation. In fact, Padre Pio came here in November, 1908, for theology studies.

We enter the church, which consists of a central nave and a smaller aisle to the left. Like Gesualdo, Sant'Egidio suffered severe damage from the 1980 earthquake and has been renovated. As we make our way through the church and convent, I note that the workmanship here is much better than in Gesualdo. Perhaps a different contractor worked here. Above the main altar is a painting of the Madonna delle Grazie, from the eighteenth century. There are more paintings of the Annunziata, the Archangel Gabriel, and one of the Virgin Mary. On the left wall is a fresco of St. Egidio (an early Roman martyr), and on the right, Christ and the Madonna.

Fra' Raffaele then takes me up to the cloister. We arrive at Padre Pio's cell, no. 3. It is marked with a framed sign hanging on the wall by the door. It says, "In this cell, from November 1908 through May, 1909, St. Pio of Pietrelcina, lived, then a student of theology." I ask Fra' Raffaele how they correctly identified this cell as belonging to Padre Pio, to which he says that Padre Pio had once told someone that his cell in Montefusco was the third room after the guardian's. The guardian's was the first, so his was number three.

We step inside. As elsewhere, the cell is outfitted with vintage furniture and relics. A habit worn by Padre Pio hangs in a standing glass encasement at the foot of the narrow bed. It, too, has an original mattress stuffed with corn husks. There is an old desk and chair with a reliquary on it.

As we are standing in the cell, I hear voices coming from the corridor. Either I'm mistaken or I hear US English with a northeastern accent. I step outside and greet an Italian guide leading a family of four. To my surprise, they're from Philadelphia. There is a grandmother, her daughter, and her two twenty-something sons. The grandmother speaks some Italian, though in dialect. I ask her if she had relatives from this region, to which she says her parents emigrated from a nearby village. She is devoted to Padre Pio and took her daughter and grandsons to visit.

After exchanging more pleasantries, Fra' Raffaele invites everyone inside the cell to pray. Then he takes the reliquary — containing some of Padre Pio's hair and a kerchief used to wipe blood — from the desk and uses it to bless us. We leave the family to pray alone and head back downstairs.

Fra' Raffaele asks me if I want to stay for lunch. I accept. I have a personal rule: never turn down a meal in an Italian monastery or convent. For good reason. They eat well. In fact, I have been smelling seafood aromas wafting throughout the convent corridors and courtyard since we arrived. Today is Friday. (The religious in Italy still observe no-meat Fridays throughout the year.)

Over lunch, which consists of spaghetti and tomato sauce with squid and octopus, I get to know the fraternity. It is made up of three friars. In addition to Fra' Raffaele, there is an Indian friar, and the guardian, Padre Marciano Guarino. Today, there are two other guests for lunch, both friars. One of them is from Lebanon, though he is stationed in the Marches where I live.

After two more courses consisting of more delicious seafood, Fra' Raffaele and I head over to the break room for a brief period of relaxation and camaraderie. Neither of us has time for the proper amount of *riposo* (rest) – at least an hour is warranted after the large meal. He has a meeting in town with a prayer group, and I need to get to Foggia. He makes me another espresso – obligatory for the drive, as the brain really does slow down after postprandial Mediterranean lunches. I thank him for his time, we say farewell, and I get in my car and program Foggia into my GPS.

Google Maps tells me that Foggia is 107 kilometers (66 mi) away and will take one hour and eighteen minutes. The route appears decent. It takes me on a state highway to a place called Candela (I've never heard of it), and then north on a straighter highway up to Foggia. It doesn't look like there is much en route, other than more small villages I've never heard of.

Apart from the route, I'm more concerned about something else. I don't have much methane left. In fact, shortly after leaving Montefusco and merging onto State Highway 7, I run out of methane and my vehicle switches automatically to unleaded gasoline. I should have 150 kilometers (90 mi) in the auxiliary 15-liter tank. However, my reserve tank was only about three quarters full to begin with. I make a conservative calculation and conclude that I have only 100 kilometers (62 mi) before I am completely out of both tanks of fuel. Since there are not many methane stations in this area – or they are exorbitantly expensive – I may have to fill up with unleaded every hour or so. I might not have a choice.

As we make our way to Foggia, I am feeling enthusiastic. By now, we have visited all but one of the convents of Padre Pio. Sant'Anna is the only remaining site. As I drive through the countryside, I reflect on my final destination. I'm headed east. So did Padre Pio. The convent and church of San Giovanni Rotondo are located at the easternmost part in their Province. I'm wondering if there is something spiritual in this. The sun rises in the East, the Holy Land is in the East, important basilicas and cathedrals are oriented toward the East. Padre Pio went east. I also consider how Foggia is on the plains, while San Giovanni Rotondo is up on the mountain. Surely there is something mystical about Padre Pio climbing up the mountain to his final destination.

As I am trying to look for spiritual meaning in my pilgrimage in the footsteps of Padre Pio, my attention begins to be diverted to something more pressing: this issue of gas. Before leaving Montefusco, I checked my app. There are no methane stations until Foggia. Though I could fill up my smaller tank with unleaded gasoline en route, I've now been driving for forty-five minutes and have not passed a single gas station. As the needle on my unleaded gauge moves left past the slighter three-eighths mark and approaches the heavier one-quarter mark, I begin to become concerned. Surely, there will be a station out here. There must be, right? I drive some more. No. There is not.

If up until now I have been romanticizing the bucolic, agrarian aspect of this remote area of Southern Italy, I now begin to reassess. A little modernity would be nice right about now. In the form of a gas station. The reality is that there is nothing around me… except land and farms. Though I know I should not feel this way, negativity and criticism begin to creep into my consciousness. Pejorative terms from my rearing in America's South flash (against my will) through my mind – boondocks, the sticks, Podunk country. I begin to wonder if the spiritual benefits of being in the middle of nowhere are outweighed by the reality of trying to conduct business in the same middle of nowhere.

I run some numbers in my head. I calculate that I should be able to make it to Foggia with the remaining gasoline in my tank. *Should* is the critical word. I feel elated when I finally pass a gas station on the other side of the four-lane highway separated by a median. I choose not to exit ahead and backtrack, assuming there must be a station on my side soon. There isn't. Instead, after another ten kilometers or so, I pass yet another gas station on the opposite side of the median. Really? I begin to wonder if there is something spiritual at work here.

Though I already began praying a while back and felt an inner sense of confidence that I would not run out of gas, I begin considering the reality that I actually might run out of gas. I remind myself that the Lord allows adverse circumstances for good reasons, and I begin to plan for what I'll do out here in the middle of nowhere if (and when) I run out. Moreover, I have had enough formation in Christian spirituality to know that we are to "bless the Lord at all times" in difficult circumstances – a trait that marks the mature Christian – and not just when things go well. I begin saying prayers of praise. This eases the worry… until the steady low fuel warning light comes on. I'm anxious again.

Finally, I pass the city sign of Foggia in black letters on a white background. I am in the city limits. By now, my tank is less than one eighth full, and my low fuel warning light is flashing. I wish it would stop flashing… Trust me, I know I am low on gas! Even though I'm in the "city" now, I again pass another gas station on the other side of the median dividing the road. Good grief.

Finally, *Deo Gratias!* I see a Q8 station in the distance… on my side of the road. My anxiety level settles down, I pull in running on fumes, and fill up my 15-liter tank with unleaded. Then I follow my app to the methane station, which is three kilometers away on the other side of Foggia and fill up that tank. (€1.82 is a decent price, too.) Now, with 550 kilometers (340 mi) worth of fuel in my two tanks, I, too, feel refueled. It's time to get on with my pilgrimage. I enter the church of Sant'Anna into my GPS and am off. It's eight minutes away.

When we arrive, I park by a green space, get out, and look around. Though to the north of the historic center of Foggia, we're still well within the urban center. I'm once again convinced that this area was rural when the Capuchins arrived centuries ago. I look up at the façade and convent, both a freshly-painted yellow. The architecture is a simple, neo-classical style with Baroque scrolls. Though I don't want to admit it, it appears ordinary, little different than any of the other numerous churches I've seen driving across town. I approach the church door, which is enclosed by a wrought iron gate. It is locked. By now it is 4:30. Shouldn't it be open?

I walk a few steps to my left to the door of the friary, ring the bell, and am buzzed in right away. I enter and note offices to my right and left, staffed by three women. I ask one of them if I can see the church. To my disappointment, I am told that the church will not open until 6:30 when Mass is celebrated. I ask if I can see a friar, but am told that they are not available. Just when I begin to feel a major letdown and open my mouth to describe what I have been through today in my journey from Pietrelcina, the woman pulls a FFP2 anti-covid mask out of her desk drawer, puts it on, and tells me to follow her. She will show me around. Praise God! (It is so much easier to praise God when things go well, I think to myself...)

As we begin up the stairs, I tell my guide that this is my final visit in my pilgrimage in the footsteps of the ten convents where Padre Pio lived, and I briefly describe some of my adventures. I note how I have been disappointed to discover that most of the Capuchin convents have been enveloped by urban expansion while centuries ago they were in rural areas.

"Like this one," I remark, attempting to show off how well I understand Capuchin history.

"Actually, Sant'Anna was built recently... that is, in 1891. The Capuchin priests returned to Foggia in 1882 after the Suppression, but were unable to recover their historic convent of Santa Maria di Costantinopoli, which was confiscated by the Kingdom of Italy. Instead, they came here and took custody of a derelict church and old house, which they transformed into the actual church and modern convent. It was already a populous neighborhood." So much for my knowledge of Capuchin history.

She leads me into the church, which has been recently renovated. It is white and well illuminated. It consists of a main central nave and a smaller aisle, or chapel, on the left. The ceiling is decorated by a lovely painting of St. Michael the Archangel, and St. Francis receiving the stigmata in Laverna. On the main altar is a wooden statue of Sant'Anna (St. Anne), the mother of Mary, holding the Christ child. My guide tells me that the statue was moved here from the old church, and there is an ancient devotion to St. Anne in these parts.

Elsewhere are statues of Padre Pio, St. Anthony, St. Elizabeth, St. Clare, and St. Ludwig. A prominent wooden crucifix adorns the wall.

As we make our way up the stairs to the cloister, we pass a series of photographs of Padre Pio as a young man. Next, we pass a hallway with a series of historic photographs depicting the transformation of Sant'Anna from its origins as a wayside church into what it is today.

Finally, we arrive at a room that is identified as Padre Pio's cell. It is notably larger than the cells in the other convents. As we enter, I consider briefly what took place here – the noises and spiritual attacks Padre Pio suffered while in the community. Once more, it consists of historic furnishings, including the familiar desk and chair, wash basin and pitcher, and mattress stuffed with corn leaves. Directly across from the cell is a chapel, also filled with relics we've seen before: vestments, an ancient statute of Jesus, gloves, shoes, sandals, socks, a kerchief, and a pen and ink well. Set within a glass encasement is a large reliquary with a similar kerchief and hair, as in Montefusco.

Having concluded our visit, as we descend the stairs, I ask my guide about the house of Raffaelina Cerase. She says it's very close and she'll point it out. We step outside on the street, turn right, make another right, and she points out a street in the distance. She tells me to turn right there and go to the church of San Giuseppe. Raffaelina's house is next to it. She says the house cannot be visited, but there is a plaque on the wall marking it.

I walk less than 300 meters to the church of San Giuseppe and recognize the otherwise nondescript house as belonging to Raffaella Cerase by the plaque. It says (in a Latinate Italian style):

> The Religious Province of the Friars Minor Capuchin
>   of Sant'Angelo and Padre Pio-Foggia
>
> In this house was born and was godly
> RAFFAELLA CERASE, a Franciscan Tertiary
> By class and virtue, a precious gem
> To whom splendor added the masterpiece
> Of her spiritual father ST. PIO DA PIETRELCINA

Who sublimed her sufferings when from [the church of] Sant'Anna
Daily he went to visit her at her house, celebrating the divine Eucharist
Nourishing her with communion, purifying her with confession
Illuminating her with counsels until she was ready for heaven.
On March 25, 1916, by now a spouse conformed to the crucified bridegroom

Foggia, 17 February 2020

I close my eyes and spend some time reflecting on this woman who lived here. Though little is known about Raffaelina Cerase, she played a pivotal role in Padre Pio returning to the order. Through her intervention, Padre Pio finally left Pietrelcina and returned to this Capuchin convent in Foggia. It was the last convent he lived in before his final destination.

As Padre Pio left Foggia, we do the same. I am exhausted due to the hassles and stresses of the day and am looking forward to the conclusion of the pilgrimage. With the sun setting behind us, we make our way east (with two full tanks of gas), in the direction of San Giovanni Rotondo.

18: In the Footsteps: San Giovanni Rotondo

As we leave the urban confines of Foggia and make our way through the rural countryside of northern Puglia toward Manfredonia, I suddenly realize we are approaching the conclusion of our journey in the footsteps of St. Padre Pio. I feel a unique blend of emotions. I am immensely grateful for all I have done and seen, for those who have accompanied me along the way, and for the friars and laypersons I have met. I have been the recipient of innumerable gifts and memories, some of which will last a lifetime. I am also exhausted. This last day has been the most stressful. Despite the fatigue, I am feeling energized by my final destination. This is one of my favorite places in the world.

Though I have made the trip up to San Giovanni Rotondo in the Gargano Mountains many times, this time feels different. I have now experienced a different side of Padre Pio. I have been to all ten convents where he lived. I have seen for myself the cells where he slept and the choirs and churches where he prayed. I have traversed this Province far and wide and traveled up and down the mountain hermitages, as he did. I feel closer to him and feel like I know him better.

As we turn left off the main road between Foggia and Manfredonia, I look up at the vast mountain plateau in front of us. We are climbing our final mountain. Though the Gargano Promontory – the spur jutting into the Adriatic Sea – is one mountain among many Padre Pio climbed, it is the largest one in the Province. It is visible as far as the eye can see from east to west.

After the third *tornante* (switchback), the terrain changes. Instead of rich, fertile soil, the land is now arid and rocky. Instead of long tracts of farmland, there are now shrubs and small trees clinging to the cliffs among crevices and sharp fissures. In addition to the healthy olive trees and prickly pear cactuses (Ita: *fichi d'india*), there are gnarled, dead tree trunks. Occasionally fatted, albino-white cows show themselves on the steep mountain slopes. Clinging to the mountainside with the dexterity of nimble mountain goats, they graze and move about effortlessly in this untamed habitat. Not far away is the wild Foresta Umbra. Some of it has never been touched by humans.

As we round the final switchback and surface at the top of the plateau, I look up at San Giovanni Rotondo, still a few kilometers away. One's perspective changes at the top of the mountain — visually, but also spiritually. Somehow Padre Pio saw in this barren land a providential site to build his hospital. While no one else would have dared do such a thing, he had the gift of being able to see with the eyes of God. I can already see the monolithic hospital on the top of the hill. Above it is the protected National Park of the Gargano including Mount Calvo, the highest peak in the range.

As we get closer to San Giovanni, we pass newly constructed residential homes interspersed with ruined farmhouses. The first roundabout is embellished with a modern artistic display and an image of Padre Pio. Grazing below the décor is a small flock of sheep under the gaze of a watchful shepherd. I smile at Padre Pio's personal welcome to his adopted city.

I arrive at my hotel, park, and exit my mud-coated vehicle (I still haven't cleaned it since my incident in San Marco la Catola). I can't help notice how different the climate is up here. It must be ten degrees cooler (15 Fahrenheit) than Foggia. The air is much more crisp. Just as Padre Pio did, I take a deep breath of the cool, salubrious mountain air.

After I check in, we make our way on foot up toward the sanctuary and hospital. As we arrive, the Sanctuary of Santa Maria delle Grazie is on the left, the hospital on the right. Whereas this land was once a barren, rocky mountain, it is now the site of a veritable "hospital city" to use the term envisaged by Padre Pio. According to the Casa Sollievo della Sofferenza website, today the hospital handles 1,200 beds for 60,000 annual admissions, 9,500 surgeries per year, and over 1.3 million annual outpatient procedures. It is one of the largest, most prestigious hospital complexes in Southern Italy and is well-regarded throughout Europe.

It is impossible to stand among the sanctuary and hospital complex operating side by side and not be struck by the dichotomy. While religion and science are sometimes cast as enemies of one another, San Giovanni Rotondo is as good as any an example of a harmony between the two. Padre Pio was not "a man of the Middle Ages" – as some accused him of being. Nor was he an adherent of positivism, as was the Franciscan priest-doctor who visited him and slandered him to the Holy Office. Instead, Padre Pio saw faith and medicine in unity when he made his famous speech one year after the inauguration of the hospital. He perceived the hospital as: "a temple of prayer and science, where humanity finds itself in Jesus Crucified as a single sheepfold, under a single shepherd." To him, faith and medicine were the proverbial seamless garment. He could have merely prayed for all those who came to him asking for cures. Instead, he was concrete and sought practical cures. He embodied the words of St. James: "What good is it, my brothers, if someone says he has faith but does not have works?" (James 2: 14).

I look at the sanctuary of Our Lady of Grace and reflect on my first visit here. I came to San Giovanni Rotondo the first time in late 2001 accompanied by my fiancée and her family. I knew very little about Padre Pio at that point in my journey. To me then, he was one saint among many. Yet, a seed was planted and it grew. Now, some twenty years later, I am a passionate devotee of Padre Pio and I have accompanied dozens of groups here. (My first experience in San Giovanni Rotondo is described in greater detail in the afterword.)

I walk into the *Chiesa Antica* (the Ancient Church) of Our Lady of Grace, as I have done countless times. But having spent the past five days exploring the Capuchin convents and churches in this Province,

I now see the ancient church of Santa Maria delle Grazie as a typical Capuchin church. It is small and composed of a main nave to the left and a smaller side aisle to the right. The nave has two recessed side altars (one of which now hosts the women's confessional), while the right-hand aisle is made up of three side altars. Above the main altar is a sixteenth-century canvas painting of Our Lady of Grace, flanked by Sts. John the Baptist and the Evangelist. As in every other Capuchin church, the choir is located above and in the rear of the church.

In and of itself, this church is just like the others within the Province of Sant'Angelo and Foggia. However, there is an enormous difference. There is a subtle glass door at the rear of the right-hand aisle leading to a much larger, modern sanctuary. This newer church does not have the aspect of a Capuchin church, though it has retained some elements. Comprised of a large nave with no transept and two side aisles, it appears more like an ancient Roman basilica. A large mosaic above the main altar is effectively a reproduction of the image of Our Lady in the ancient church. The only aspect that reminds me we are in a Capuchin church is the choir located above the church in the rear. This is the newer church built during Padre Pio's lifetime for the ever larger crowds.

But the farthest departure from Capuchin architecture is captured in the sprawling, ultramodern church located just around the corner. Designed by the world-renowned Italian architect, Renzo Piano, and completed as recently as 2004, it is known as the Padre Pio Pilgrimage Church. Inside are dazzling mosaics executed by Jesuit priest, Fr. Marko Rupnik, and his team. The ramp leading down to the crypt depicts scenes from the life of Padre Pio on one side corresponding to comparable scenes from the life of St. Francis on the other. The crypt is decorated with golden mosaics depicting entirely the life of Christ.

The newest church was designed to contain the body of Padre Pio. In 2008, his sarcophagus was opened and his remains were translated here. But this church is so radically different from the other two (locals refer to it as a sports stadium), the friars decided to occasionally relocate Padre Pio's body temporarily back to the old church. During the winter months, from late November through March, his remains are brought back to the crypt beneath Our Lady of Grace. Many people consider Our Lady of Grace to be the true center and heart of San Giovanni Rotondo. I do, too. It feels more like Padre Pio. It feels like home.

I take some time to explore the complex again. Little has changed since I made my first pilgrimage here two decades ago. After visiting the ancient church and sacristy, I go down to the crypt and follow the corridor within the ancient convent open to the public. The visit includes the choir where Padre Pio received the stigmata and cell no. 1 where he died. The same relics and rooms are on display, and San Giovanni Rotondo has changed little since I was here the first time.

Outside, the House of Relief of Suffering is still bustling with patients and medical staff. Guided visits throughout the sanctuary complex continue, though they are now more organized, and the hospital is now open for guided visits. The Stations of the Cross (Via Crucis) leading up the hillside, inaugurated in 1981, haven't changed either. The house of Mary Pyle, the American benefactress and spiritual daughter of Padre Pio, was there just downhill toward the valley, but was not open to the public. It is now. There is a new wax museum, though I haven't been.

On the other hand, this place was radically different one century ago. Old black and white photographs displayed on the walls of hotels and coffee bars reveal a forlorn church and convent set in a rocky landscape. When I look at those pictures, I am reminded of Scripture. I think of the narrative of Mary and her Magnificat (see Luke 1:46-55). Just as God chose the humble Jewish girl of backwater Nazareth for the Annunciation, he has again chosen the obscure places, ignored by the world, to make his face shown. God did not choose the great, he chose the meek. He shows his attention to the poor and lowly whom he lifts up.

With my back to the sanctuary, I look down and see the old village of San Giovanni in the distance. One hundred years ago, this road was little more than a narrow mule track. Today it is a busy thoroughfare lined with hotels, restaurants, and souvenir shops.

While modernity has crept up on all the Capuchin convents in this Province, the change is most dramatic here.

If the contemporary history of San Giovanni Rotondo is one of radical change, it is due exclusively to the holiness, vision, and works of St. Pio of Pietrelcina. The city boasts at once one of the most important hospitals in Southern Italy and one of the most visited religious sites in all of Christendom. Due to visitors coming for pilgrimage, tourism, and medical care, it is estimated that some six million people venture here annually (before the pandemic). San Giovanni Rotondo is no longer an obscure village; it is a thriving pilgrimage and medical center. The *Sangiovannesi* are no longer provincial farmers and herders; they are now business owners who work with people from all over the world.

Infinitely more important than the material gains are the innumerable spiritual transformations that have taken place here. They began with Padre Pio himself. He who was the child, Francesco Forgione from Pietrelcina, became a priest. The priest received the stigmata transforming him into a walking crucified Christ. He recalls the New Man in Scripture: "So whoever is in Christ is a new creation: the old things have passed away; behold, new things have come" (2 Cor 5:17). He offered his sufferings to humanity for conversions and healings. And they abounded. When Padre Pio arrived, countless souls came first from the village and later from all over the world. They were transformed by his Masses, confessions, or simply by watching him. People whose lives were disfigured by sin and disordered living underwent dramatic conversions.

And still they come. People continue to arrive from the world over and they still turn to him for intercession. They suffer from every form of spiritual and physical sickness and they seek relief. And many still receive graces. Padre Pio used to say, "In the tomb I will be more alive than ever!;" and, "I will make more noise after my death." True to his word, he continues to make himself heard.

I meet my friend, Sr. Maria Villani. She is not a nun; rather, she is a vowed consecrated virgin. She wears a full habit, but lives alone in an apartment here in San Giovanni Rotondo. She is originally from a village not far away. When she was a child, 300 people from her town walked through the night thirty kilometers (20 mi) to San Giovanni Rotondo on pilgrimage. She recalls how she became separated from her family, but had a vision of Padre Pio who consoled her. She felt her vocation on that day.

Sr. Maria introduced me to Fra' Raffaele Armiento, the friar now stationed in Montefusco. Before the pandemic, she and he accompanied me into the private section of the convent here in San Giovanni Rotondo. I ask her if we can go again. To my disappointment, she says it is not possible. No amount of prayer or begging will make a difference. Due to the pandemic, the friars have enacted strict measures. No one can go in – not even her or even other Capuchin friars from other Provinces.

I recall my visit in detail. The convent is very similar to the other Capuchin convents in this Province. It consists of the *stanza del fuoco* – the community fireplace room with a hearth, also retrofitted with antique furnishings. Then there is the refectory where Padre Pio took his meals, although he rarely ate. The two places where he sat are identified with a metal plate. The highlight of the visit was cell no. 5 where Padre Pio lived most of his life. It houses two important relics – an undershirt Padre Pio wore beneath his habit, signed by traces of blood on the right shoulder, and the most remarkable relic of Padre Pio (aside from his body): Padre Pio's heart. It remains in cell no. 5, except for extraordinary circumstances, when it is sent elsewhere for devotion by the faithful.

I say good night to Sr. Maria, and make my way back to my hotel. The next morning, we attend Mass together at 6:30 AM. Afterwards, we walk through the church and talk. As we do, she comes across people she knows. One of them is a well-dressed, elderly man who is deaf and mute. She gestures for him to show me "the photograph." He reaches into his jacket pocket and hands me a worn, laminated black and white photo. Sr. Maria tells me it was taken on the day of Padre Pio's funeral. Behind his coffin is a crowd of men. With a delightful smile, the gentleman points to a young man in the photo and then to himself. A few moments later, we meet another elderly woman with whom Sr. Maria stops and converses with privately. As we exit the church, Sr. Maria tells me that the elderly people who knew Padre Pio always come to the 6:30 Mass. Then they go home and pray for the rest of the day. They were trained by *il Padre*.

As we walk toward the old sacristy, Sr. Maria tells stories. While passing through the new church of Santa Maria delle Grazie, she recounts an episode regarding a spiritual daughter of Padre Pio who died about ten years ago. She points to the seats to the left of the main altar and says this is where his spiritual sons and daughters used to sit for Mass. Just as this spiritual daughter was about to receive communion, she had a strong vision of Padre Pio in her mind. Suddenly, she recalled an unconfessed sin. She refrained from receiving communion and went straight to confession after Mass.

After we visit the old sacristy, we enter the ancient church and go to the chapel of St. Francis, the first one in the right-hand aisle. Sr. Maria tells another anecdote about a different spiritual daughter she knew, also deceased. Up until her death some years back, this woman would come to the chapel of St. Francis each morning and wipe the altar railing with kerchiefs. Skeptical, Sr. Maria asked why she did that.

"*Tu non capisci niente*" (You don't understand anything), the elderly spiritual daughter told the young Sr. Maria. She said that she witnessed countless drops of the "Blood of Christ" spilled out on this altar. Padre Pio frequently celebrated Mass here before the construction of the newer church, and his spiritual daughters would sit just inside the altar railing.

"This altar rail is holy," she told Sr. Maria.

We continue walking and talking. Sr. Maria tells me that Padre Pio used to say that if we want to know what true charity is, we should stand below the cross. He showed with his actions what charity was and with his body what the cross was. His life was his teaching. He showed us the face of God. Even if we will never have the spiritual gifts he had, we can learn from him as disciples and seek to imitate him. We, too, can offer our sufferings for others, especially for our children – if we are parents or grandparents. We, too, can pray the rosary daily and go to Mass frequently.

I take the time to ask Sr. Maria about something that has been on my mind. There are countless reports of people who received graces and miracles through the intercession of Padre Pio. But what about those who asked for healing and never received it.

Without hesitation, Sr. Maria mentions a man named Pietro who died not long ago. Padre Pio called him Pietruccio (little Peter). He was a spiritual son and the two loved one another very much. Pietruccio was blind. When he was young, he went to Padre Pio and asked if he would heal him of his blindness. He responded by asking Pietruccio if he wanted to be saved or have his eyesight.

"I want to be saved."

"Then you will never see."

When we ask for miracles, we do so based on what we believe is for our own good. God, however, knows what is ultimately good for us. Sometimes, the reception of a miracle may lead to something other than an increase in virtue and charity. It may even lead to our downfall. God, who knows the future, knows if a healing or certain miracle will benefit us or not. Padre Pio, too, had this insight. He knew when to ask for a miracle and when not to.

While many of Padre Pio's spiritual sons and daughters were reserved and lived quiet, hidden lives, some have composed their own written testimonies. Their writings are treasure troves into the spirituality and teachings of Padre Pio. They pierce the inner life of Padre Pio in a way journalists and biographers cannot, as they offer unparalleled insight into Pio's mind, heart, and spirit.

Sr. Maria says that as Padre Pio was aging, his spiritual sons and daughters worried what they would do after his passing. They asked him to whom they should go when he was no longer with them. His answer was striking: "Go before the tabernacle: in Jesus you will find me." While such a statement may appear to border on blasphemy, Padre Pio did not speak out of pride. He was being humble. He was revealing his profound love of God and gratitude for what God had done in this life. God had made Padre Pio like himself. Padre Pio incarnated the words of St. Paul: "I live, no longer I, but Christ lives in me" (Gal 2:20). If ever any saint had become fully divinized in this life, it was St. Padre Pio.

19: In the Footsteps: St. Michael and Beyond

I cannot in good conscience conclude our journey in the footsteps of St. Pio of Pietrelcina without one final visit: the Sanctuary of Monte Sant'Angelo – located on the Adriatic Sea about twenty-five kilometers (15 mi) from San Giovanni Rotondo. As the pilgrims on the Spanish Camino de Santiago – the Way of St. James – arrive at their goal in Compostela, Spain, that is the sanctuary housing the remains of St. James the Great, and continue a little farther to Finisterre ("the end of the world") on the Atlantic Ocean, we, too, make our way out to Monte Sant'Angelo on the sea.

Monte Sant'Angelo is an important pilgrimage site due to the apparition of St. Michael the Archangel who appeared in a grotto at least four times in the Middle Ages. Monte Sant'Angelo became an important sanctuary and coveted pilgrimage site especially in the era of the Crusades. It served as a stopover point for crusaders and pilgrims alike venturing out from Europe to the Holy Land... and returning. Unlike Finisterre on the Atlantic Ocean, the medieval people knew what lay beyond in the Mediterranean Sea (its name means "middle of the world"). They also knew of the dangers. Speaking to this are handprints traced into the walls. Legends say that before departing, pilgrims would trace their right hand in the wall; if they returned, they would trace the other. Sadly, there are many more lone handprints than pairs.

Padre Pio's devotion to St. Michael is well documented. He was fiercely devoted to the archangel throughout his life, and he visited the sanctuary at least once. The angelic world was real to him, and he communicated with his guardian angel since childhood. He frequently sent people to Monte Sant'Angelo as penance to make satisfaction for their sins.

Padre Pio wasn't alone in his devotion to the archangel. Now having walked in the footsteps of St. Padre Pio, I have seen for myself the intense devotion to the warrior angel in this territory. I have observed almost as many images of St. Michael as of Padre Pio: a winged St. Michael dressed for combat stands with his foot on the demon, his right hand raised with sword, ready to strike. The history books say that the bellicose Lombards brought their devotion to St. Michael – to whom they would pray before battle – when they settled here in the early Middle Ages. Still today, St. Michael is frequently invoked by modern warriors – exorcists in their struggle against demons.

The name derives from Hebrew, *Mikha'el*. It is more a question than a common name. Moreover, it is a response. The name translates into English as: "Who is like God?" St. Michael's question is his reaction to Lucifer – the beautiful angel of light who wanted to be like God, rebelled, and was cast out. Michael retained his humility and forever served God by stating, through a question, that there is no one like God – not even the highest archangels.

As we leave San Giovanni Rotondo, just past the old cemetery (where St. Padre Pio's parents are buried), the road becomes, once more, tortuous and desolate. And yet it has, once again, an inviting lure. All around are flocks of grazing cattle, farmland, and ubiquitous limestone rocks strewn throughout the fields and built into rough, mortarless fences. A priest I know from this region, Don Domenico Affortunato, says that when God finished creating the world, he deposited his leftover stones in Puglia. The rocks and scenery remind me of the landscape in Croatia on the way to Medjugorje. In fact, geologists say that the coast of Puglia was once joined to the Dalmatian coast of Croatia and Albania. Millions of years ago, there was no Adriatic Sea. The sea is the result of a fault line. As evidence, there are similar unique fruit and nut trees native to Puglia and Albania.

Just over thirty minutes from San Giovanni Rotondo, we climb our last mountain and wind our way up the switchbacks to the top of Monte Sant'Angelo. As we do, I feel overwhelmed by all I have experienced.

I cannot help but reflect on Padre Pio. I am thinking specifically of his Province. The fact is that there are no longer enough friars to staff the convents. When young Pio entered the order, it was expanding. The friars were reclaiming convents closed due to the Suppression. Young men were pouring into the order. There was even a wait list to enter. Now the Province is in decline. Actually, it is dying. This was clearly on the minds of everyone I came into contact with. The friars, priests, and laity are all concerned with a shortage of vocations. One of the friars lamented that there have been ten funerals so far this year. And there are just a handful of young men in formation. They are clearly living the Paschal Mystery.

The form of life has changed, too. The Capuchins are no longer hermits. Nor are they penitents. I do not dare blame them. The modern world encroached on them and their lives. Whereas their convents and churches were strategically placed out in the countryside or in the hills for solitude, they are now situated in the center of busy suburbs. The needs of the Church are different, too. Since there are fewer priests everywhere, those left are called to more ministries. Consequently, Capuchin priests frequently staff parish churches in addition to their own. Much of their time is spent in their cars serving the pastoral needs of the people.

We arrive at the top of the mountain and I park in the large lot above the old city of Monte Sant'Angelo. I make my way to the edge of the parking lot where I stand and gaze out to the southeast, marveling at the wine-blue waters of the Mediterranean Sea. Though not visible, in the distance are Greece, Turkey, and the Holy Land. After asking St. Michael for protection, pilgrims of old would sail these waters. They would embark across the Adriatic Sea and arrive in Durres in today's western Albania. Then they would continue on the land route across the mountainous Greek peninsula to Thessalonica, Alexandria, Constantinople, Ankara in modern Turkey, and then turn south, passing through Damascus, finally arriving in

Jerusalem. Some would sail all the way from Brindisi, in southern Italy, to Acre, the crusader city in today's northern Israel, and walk down to Jerusalem from there.

We pass by Monte Sant'Angelo's crusader-era castle with its massive tower, ramparts, thick walls, and dry moat, and start downhill. Over the centuries, countless popes, saints, royalty, and commoners have come here to visit this storied shrine. After St. Michael appeared to a farmer in the year 493, the local bishop ordered three days of prayer and fasting. Then St. Michael appeared to the bishop. At the third apparition, the archangel told the bishop to build a chapel, but not to consecrate it because it would be consecrated "with my presence." This is the only church in Christendom not consecrated by human hands. For this reason, the Sanctuary of Monte Sant'Angelo is known as the Celestial Basilica.

After descending past some souvenir shops and coffee bars, we arrive at the entrance to the basilica. Over the door in large block letters is a Latin inscription: "TERRIBILIS EST LOCUS ISTE; HIC DOMUS DEI EST ET PORTA COELI" (This is a terrible place; Here is the house of God and the door of Heaven). After passing through the door – known as the "gateway to heaven" – the atmosphere changes. There is a long, dark, musty descent down eighty-six stone stairs. Some say it is suggestive of Jacob's Ladder, where angels go up and down (see Genesis 28:10–19). Along the stairway, there are frequent statues and icons of St. Michael with his sword raised in battle and his foot on the head of a dragon or demon. There are scriptural references to St. Michael from the Books of Daniel and Revelation.

Just before entering the grotto, on the right is a nondescript altar with an image of a friar kneeling. Underneath it is a small glass panel covering a TAU cross incised into the rock. Guides say it was carved by St. Francis. When he visited this sanctuary, this is as far as the saint from Assisi went. He did not feel worthy enough to enter the grotto. (Aware of my own limitations), I humbly enter.

I sit down, quiet myself, and allow the cool, cavernous grotto to speak to me. An exorcist priest I know believes this cave and the sanctuary of St. Padre Pio in San Giovanni Rotondo are among the holiest places in the world. He feels the presence of the angel here. I do not have the charismatic gifts he possesses, but I do feel the presence of the divine here.

I give thanks to God for bringing me here safely, for giving me the gift of this pilgrimage, and for blessing me with my wife and children. I open my online bible in my cellphone app and read from Scripture about St. Michael: "Michael and his angels battled against the dragon. The dragon and its angels fought back, but they did not prevail and there was no longer any place for them in heaven (Revelation 12: 7-8). I say the Prayer to St. Michael followed by the Chaplet of St. Michael.

I ask one of the Polish monks in service in the rear of the grotto for a prayer of consecration. I go around to the back of the cave where St. Michael appeared. There I consecrate each of my family members to God through St. Michael, especially my youngest child, Michael. I bring all my personal intentions to the intercession of St. Michael, St. Francis, and St. Padre Pio. I pray for vocations and holy families, for peace in Eastern Europe and throughout the world, for my children, for the souls of my relatives, for an end to the pandemic and , for the conversion of souls in Europe and the United States, and for other personal intentions.

As I arise from the grotto back into the daylight, I do so with renewed faith and hope. These past five days have been like an abbreviated Christian journey in which I have experienced the Paschal Mystery. My pilgrimage consisting of some little penances here and there certainly does not compare with Padre Pio who lived Christ's life, death, and resurrection physically and spiritually in his body and soul for half a century. Nonetheless, these small sacrifices I made remind me of the great sacrifice Christ made on the cross, and what it leads to: "If, then, we have died with Christ, we believe that we shall also live with him" (Romans 6:8). For, "the sufferings of this present time are as nothing compared with the glory to be revealed for us" (Romans 8:18).

As I make my way back up to the parking lot at the top of the mountain, I feel a strong sense of peace. It is more like an illumination. I feel an assurance that God is with us, that he has great love for us. In an instant, all my doubts vanish. The reality that many of the orders are in decline here and so many churches are empty suddenly takes on new meaning. I feel convicted that not only will God lead us as a Church and as a people through all the challenges we are facing today, but that the path forward is precisely through the dying we are experiencing.

This is the Paschal Mystery. It is the heart of Christianity. Christ suffered, died, and rose again. God's grace is bestowed on us not despite suffering and death, but precisely because of them. The great saints like Padre Pio offer us a glimpse of this mystery. Though there will be suffering, there will be consolation. Though there will be death, there will be the Resurrection.

My pilgrimage into the Paschal Mystery is complete. May we never fear the suffering and death that are part of the Christian journey. For glory awaits us. May Padre Pio be our example and guide. Praise God forever!

Photographs Part II

Figure 13 Here in Piana Romana, Padre Pio received the "invisible stigmata" on September 7, 1910. The site was originally in the open fields beneath an elm tree. Now it is a chapel (Pietrelcina, Campania)

Figure 14 A relic of Padre Pio in the cell (Montefusco, Campania)

Figure 15 The house of Raffaellina Cerase, the noblewoman to whom Padre Pio offered spiritual assistance. She was partly responsible for bringing Padre Pio back into the order (Foggia, Puglia)

Figure 16 The facade of the ancient church of Santa Maria delle Grazie buttressed up against the newer one as they appear today (San Giovanni Rotondo, Puglia)

Figure 17 An early 20th-century photograph of the ancient church and friary of Santa Maria delle Grazie (San Giovanni Rotondo, Puglia)

Figure 18 The interior of the ancient church (San Giovanni Rotondo, Puglia)

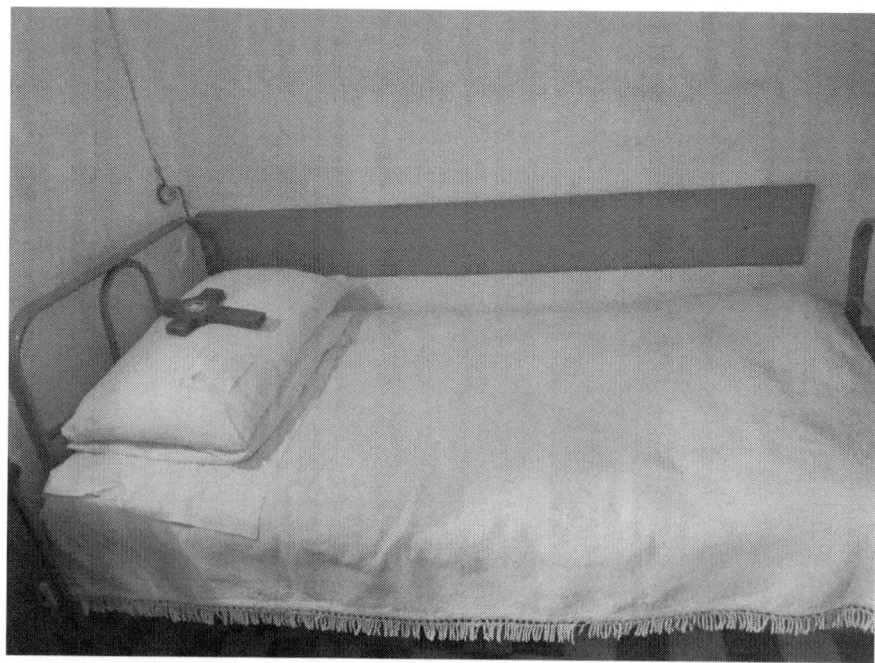

Figure 19 Padre Pio's bed in Cell no. 5, where he lived most of his life (San Giovanni Rotondo, Puglia)

Figure 20 The heart of Padre Pio is conserved in a reliquary in Cell no. 5 (San Giovanni Rotondo, Puglia)

Figure 21 Padre Pio is interred within the crypt of the modern church.

Figure 22 The crucifix through which Padre Pio received the permanent stigmata on September 20, 1918 (San Giovanni Rotondo, Puglia)

Figure 23 The body of Padre Pio is conserved within the crypt of the modern church (San Giovanni Rotondo, Puglia)

Figure 24 The grotto where St. Michael appeared in the Middle Ages (Monte Sant'Angelo, Puglia)

Afterword

I discovered Padre Pio when I visited the region of Puglia in Southern Italy for a volunteer experience in 1994. As a non-Catholic at the time, I had never heard of him. But it was impossible not to take notice of the stigmatized Capuchin whose image was everywhere. He often appeared next to St. Mary and St. John beneath crucifixes in the region's ubiquitous roadside shrines, known as aedicules. Virtually every church had at least one icon or statue of Padre Pio on a wall or in the vestibule. Yet he also surfaced in non-religious settings. Whether in a coffee bar or restaurant, automotive garage, doctor's office, or even on the side of tractor trailers, he was ubiquitous. Everyone in Puglia seemed to love Padre Pio. It is still the same today.

I came to San Giovanni Rotondo the first time with my fiancée and my future in-laws on a casual visit in 2001. Katia is from a town in Puglia called Mottola, near the port city of Taranto. I had converted to the faith not too many years earlier, and was still largely ignorant of the life of this up and coming saint and was curious. Katia's brother, Mimmo – an Italian Air Force officer – was stationed then at the military base of Amendola, halfway between Foggia and San Giovanni. He and his wife had a newborn son and chose to live in San Giovanni Rotondo, partly out of devotion to Padre Pio, partly due to the schools and hospital.

After a plentiful Sunday lunch – mandatory in those parts – we lumbered around the old part of town and then went to "see Padre Pio." When we arrived at the sanctuary, we began our visit to the ancient church of Our Lady of Grace. Mimmo and his wife, Anna, showed us around. There was a lot of activity as Padre Pio had recently been beatified and his canonization was imminent. We were shown the altars where he celebrated Mass and the sacristy where he vested and washed his hands in the ancient lavabo.

Then we crossed over to the newer church. Buttressed against the ancient church, it was built in 1956. During my first visit, Padre Pio's body was still interred in the crypt beneath the sanctuary. (The sprawling megachurch built to contain his remains in perpetuity had yet to be conceived.) I recall being struck by the crowds of people praying fervently and weeping at his tomb. Though the Church had not yet declared Padre Pio a saint, the people already had.

We then walked along a corridor displaying black and white photographs of scenes from Padre Pio's childhood in Pietrelcina: his childhood home, his parents in their old age, and the church of Sant'Anna where he received his first sacraments. After climbing two flights of stairs, we visited a room filled with vestments and liturgical vessels used by Padre Pio. There was an entire wall lined with rows of letters written to him in one year alone. As we made our way through another corridor leading to a section of the ancient friary, I recall being struck by a life-size black and white photograph of a young Padre Pio standing and revealing his stigmatized hands. The wounds were clearly visible and appeared as dark holes on the top of both hands.

Then we approached cell no. 1, where Padre Pio died early on the morning of September 23, 1968. The room was left as it was the day he died. In addition to medical devices such as a wheelchair and oxygen mask and tank, the rest of the cell contained what one would expect to find in a holy friar's cell: images of the Sacred Heart, Mary, and saints; crucifixes and a rosary; a nightstand with more devotional items; and a simple desk and chair for study and writing.

Finally, we filed through the choir above the ancient church. I recall seeing the wooden crucifix, from which a "celestial personage" impressed on his hands and feet the wounds of the permanent stigmata in an ecstatic, bloody moment. It was impossible not to remain struck by that space.

Before leaving, we meandered through the labyrinthine complex in search of the English-speaking office (in my honor). We met a gentleman named Robert from North Carolina who opened a drawer and removed a brown, fingerless glove carefully preserved in a plastic covering. He allowed me and my future wife to hold it and ask for Padre Pio's intercession over our upcoming nuptials. Then we left.

Looking back, my first venture to San Giovanni Rotondo left me with more questions than answers. I harbored a degree of skepticism, especially regarding the matter-of-fact statements about the otherworldly phenomena. Though I could accept the stigmata, I was unsure about some of the reported miracles – particularly the physical bouts with the demons. Some of what I heard seemed exaggerated or even smacked of fanaticism.

At that point in my spiritual journey, Padre Pio was a statue up on the shelf in a gift shop where I was perfectly content to leave him. Everything I learned that day was interesting, but "extra" so to speak. It didn't add anything to my faith life. I had the Eucharist and the Mass, my prayer life, and the catechism and popes for guidance. There were countless holy men and women up and down the Italian peninsula and throughout the Catholic world, and Padre Pio was one more saint.

This would soon change. Padre Pio was about to intervene in my life directly and powerfully on three separate occasions. Then I, too, would counted myself as one of his most fervent devotees.

Not long after my first visit to San Giovanni Rotondo, Padre Pio appeared to me in a dream. I was asleep in my bedroom with my back to the door. In a dreamlike state, I recognized the presence of a bearded, robed friar standing over me. He wanted to touch my hand. As I was lying on my right side, I held up my left hand. But the friar said, "No. Your right." So I extended my right hand, which he touched. Then I was fully awake. I knew it was Padre Pio.

A few years later, my parish in the U.S. hosted an exposition of a collection of first-class relics known as the Treasures of the Church. During the introduction, Fr. Carlos Martins, the founder of the ministry, invited those in attendance to locate the relic of a saint to whom we had a devotion. He said to hold the relic to our heart and see if the saint spoke to us in any way. I perused the hall and was drawn to several relics, including Sts. Francis, Clare, and Anthony of Padua. Though I am a professed member of the Secular Franciscan Order, I did not experience anything out of the ordinary through them. Then I came upon a relic of Padre Pio. I recalled the dream I had had not much earlier as I picked up his relic. No sooner did I touch it to my chest than I felt an electric-like jolt that jarred my entire body. It was a physical sensation of pressure and power accompanied by a warm feeling of consolation and well-being. It was so strong I pulled the relic away.

Padre Pio spoke to me a third time about ten years later. I was in San Giovanni Rotondo to meet one of his last living spiritual sons, Adolfo Affatato. I arrived at the Sanctuary of Santa Maria delle Grazie about thirty minutes before the 11:00 Mass, which we planned to attend together. I went into the ancient church for prayer. It was during the winter months, and there was only one other person present seated on the first bench by the main altar. I sat in the rear, near the women's confessional, where I prayed. Several minutes after I sat down, I was overwhelmed with the fragrance of roses. There was no mistaking it. It was clearly the scent of flowers.

Just before 11:00, Adolfo arrived with his wife and a friend of hers, and we went into the larger sanctuary. During the liturgy of the Eucharist, precisely the moment in which the priest elevated the host at consecration, I was again struck by the fragrance of roses. It was just as powerful as before. As if to confirm what I was experiencing, I leaned over to Adolfo and asked if his wife or her friend, both seated behind us, were wearing a rose-scented perfume. But Adolfo just smiled and said, "Don't ever doubt the gifts of Padre Pio!" I asked him if he smelled the fragrance of roses. He responded that he did not, that it was a gift for me and me alone.

After that third encounter with Padre Pio, I understood the intense devotion so many people have toward him. Over the years, I have heard many stories similar to mine – that Padre Pio has spoken to them in a powerful way through dreams or the fragrance of flowers. I realized that he wanted to tell me something. Just as we have guardian angels, we have guardian saints. Mine is Padre Pio.

Before he died, Padre Pio said, "I belong to everyone. Now everyone can say: 'Padre Pio is mine.'" Glorified in heaven, he is available to everyone as an intercessor. He is not limited to those who knew him or who have had an experience through his spiritual presence. He is there, ever desirous to continue making "more noise from heaven than from earth."

Figure 25 Padre Pio, pray for us!

For Further Reading

*Padre Pio of Pietrelcina * Letters*, Volumes I, II, and III. Second Edition, 1984, edited by Melchiorre of Pobladura and Alessandro of Ripabottoni; English Version edited by Father Gerardo Di Flumeri, O.F.M. Cap. Published by Edizioni Padre Pio da Pietrelcina SRL.

Padre Pio, Il Cammino di un Santo by Stefano Campanella. Second Edition. Published by Edizioni Padre Pio da Pietrelcina, SRL, 2021.

Padre Pio of Pietrelcina, Everybody's Cyrenean by Father Alessandro da Ripabottoni. Translated by Geraldine Nolan, Published by Edizioni Padre Pio da Pietrelcina, SRL. Reprint 2012.

Padre Pio: The True Story by Bernard Ruffin. Published by Our Sunday Visitor, 2018.

The Holy Souls: "Viva Padre Pio" by Father Alessio Parente O.F.M Cap. Published by National Centre for Padre Pio, 1994.

Send Me Your Guardian Angel by Fr. Alessio Parente O.F.M. Cap. Published by Our Lady of Grace Capuchin Friary, 1984.

Books by Author

Saint Francis of Assisi: Passion, Poverty and the Man Who Transformed the Church. Published by TAN Books, 2016.

Saint Clare of Assisi: Light From the Cloister. Published by TAN Books, 2017.

A Knight and a Lady: A Journey into the Spirituality of Saints Francis and Clare. Published by Icona Press, 2020.

The Pandemic of Padre Pio: Disciple of Our Lady of Sorrows. Written by Stefano Campanella, translated by Bret Thoman. Published by Icona Press, 2021.

St. Maria Goretti: A Journey into Forgiveness and Redemption. Published by Icona Press, 2021.

From Worldly Princess to the Foot of the Cross: The Life and Writings of Saint Camilla Battista Varano. Published by Icona Press, 2021.

Did this book help you in some way? If so, I'd love to hear about it. Sincere reviews on **Amazon** and **Goodreads** help readers find the right book they are looking for.

All of Bret Thoman's books are available on Amazon at:
www.amazon.com/Bret-Thoman/e/B0753K2PTJ

About the Author

Bret Thoman, OFS lives in Loreto, Italy with his wife and three children. He has been a member of the Secular Franciscan Order (Third Order of St. Francis) since 2003. He has a master's degree in Italian from Middlebury College, a BA from the University of Georgia in foreign languages, and a certificate in Franciscan Studies. Bret is an FAA-licensed pilot and has logged over 3,500 hours of flight time.

Bret's main activity is organizing pilgrimages for St. Francis Pilgrimages, the company he founded in 2004.
www.stfrancispilgrimages.com

Bret leads individuals and groups through Italy. He can organize and accompany groups, small and large, to the friaries of Padre Pio. He can be contacted at: bret@stfrancispilgrimages.com.

Made in the USA
Middletown, DE
31 January 2023

23641574R00135